JUNGIAN SANDPLAY

Sandplay is an increasingly popular Jungian therapy. Developed in England by Margaret Lowenfeld and in Switzerland by Dora Kalff, it knows no barriers of age, gender or language, and by allowing non-verbal articulation it adds considerably to the material available to the analyst.

Joel Ryce-Menuhin, who trained with Dora Kalff, is the leading exponent of sandplay in Britain. In this engaging book he draws upon twenty years' experience in using this method of therapy to show how children and adults of all ages and backgrounds can benefit from Jungian sandplay therapy. He expresses his deep convictions about the healing of pathology, neurosis and grief through sandplay, and describes how he incorporated sandplay into his work as a non-verbal technique to help patients express 'beyond words and before words' the deepest archetypal images projected from the unconscious. At the heart of the book are four case studies, illustrating the range and effectiveness of sandplay in its human clinical dimension, and including a moving account of a woman's healing from grief, separation and mourning in sandplay.

A former concert pianist, **Joel Ryce-Menuhin** is now a Jungian analyst. He first introduced Jungian sandplay therapy to Britain. He is the editor of *Harvest*, the journal of the C.G. Jung Analytical Psychology Club, London, and the author of *The Self in Early Childhood*.

JUNGIAN SANDPLAY

The wonderful therapy

Joel Ryce-Menuhin

London and New York

First published 1992
by Routledge
11 New Fetter Lane, London EC4P 4EE

Simultaneously published in the USA and Canada
by Routledge
a division of Routledge, Chapman and Hall, Inc.
29 West 35th Street, New York, NY 10001

Printed in Great Britain
by Mackays of Chatham PLC, Chatham, Kent

British Library Cataloguing in Publication Data
Ryce-Menuhin, Joel.
Jungian sandplay : the wonderful therapy
1. Play therapy
I. Title
615.89

Library of Congress Cataloging in Publication Data
Ryce-Menuhin, Joel
Jungian sandplay : the wonderful therapy / Joel Ryce-Menuhin.
p.   cm.
Includes bibliographical references.
Includes index.
1. Sandplay—Therapeutic use. 2. Jung, C. G. (Carl Gustav),
1875–1961.   I. Title.
[DNLM: 1. Jung, C. G. (Carl Gustav), 1875–1961. 2. Play Therapy.
3. Psychoanalytic Therapy—methods.   WM 450 R991j]
RC489.S25R93   1991
616.89'1653—dc20
DNLM/DLC
for Library of Congress

ISBN 0–415–04775–7
0–415–04776–5 (pbk)

Dedicated to my colleagues of the International Society
for Sandplay Therapy (Founder: Dora Kalff) – in
solidarity

Sand is the earth – it is at the borderline between the unseen, unconscious depths of the sea and the consciously protruding landscape. It marks the footprints of time. It marks the cosmic tides, that motion between dynamic being and empty stillness. Sand castles have captured the imagination of children and of adults as long as human beings have sought the shore.

Joel Ryce-Menuhin

CONTENTS

Acknowledgements   ix

1 AT THE THRESHOLD   1
The author's experience when he first approached
a sandbox, leading to a brief explanatory history
of this therapy.

2 THE ENTRANCE HALL   8
Playing to live. The universal psychology of play and
symbol described. The importance of freedom from
technical restraints in sandplay. How unconscious
projection reads out in sandplay interpretation.

3 INTO THE RECEPTION ROOM   28
Ritual in sandplay therapy. Projection of self as theory.
Jungian approaches. Description of materials and
sandplay room extended. Author's concepts of ritual
vis-à-vis therapist's holding presence and transference/
counter-transference.

4 WORKING IN THE SANDPLAY ROOM   38
Four case studies, the heart of the work, illustrating range and
effectiveness of sandplay in its human clinical dimension.
  1 *The story of John: A man matures in time to avoid*
    a midlife crisis.   39
  2 *The story of Clive: A young man is healed of traumatic*
    childhood ego damage.   45
  3 *The story of Marie: A mature woman in grief works*
    through her mourning process.   66
  4 *The story of Agnes: A young girl enters puberty*
    as her parents divorce.   77

5 PASSING BY THE AUTHOR'S STUDY ROOM   91

*The first mapping of sandplay forms – author's original
    and controversial new theory of the psyche as it
    maps into the sand.*   91

*Sandplay as diagnostic – diagnostic use for cancer
    in a Milan children's hospital.*   97

*Free-wheeling uses of sandplay – dialogue in sandplay
    (with therapist and between the one and the many);
    group sandplay; Jung's psychology as the parameter
    of sandplay.*   102

The universality of sandplay and its further shores.   105

Epilogue   107
Basic sandplay equipment   109
Guidelines for training to become a Sandplay Therapist   110
The Lowenfeld–Kalff correspondence   112
Note on Ryce-Menuhin's British Sandplay Group   116
References   117
Name index   120
Subject index   122

ACKNOWLEDGEMENTS

I wish to express my debt of gratitude to the Founding Members of the International Society of Sandplay Therapy (Founder: Dora Kalff) whose professional friendliness inspired me to want to write a book about sandplay. Without the two hundred sessions with the late Dora Kalff, the Jungian world pioneer and authority on sandplay as I use it, my psychological work would be bereft of my experiential knowledge and enthusiasm for the therapeutic power of sandplay. I want particularly to thank Jungian analysts, Dr Andreina Navone and Dr Paola Carducci of Rome for sharing an English translation of the cancer sandplay studies of their professionally qualified pupils of the ISST whose work I have referred to in Chapter 5.

Geoffrey Carton, the painter and graphic designer, has supplied the diagrams for Chapters 1 and 5 for which I am most grateful. Quotations from my book, *The Self in Early Childhood* published by Free Association Books, London (1988), are in my copyright. The estate of Margaret Lowenfeld has kindly supplied me with the Lowenfeld–Kalff correspondence for reference in the Appendix.

The manuscript was typed by Charlotte Keech, a most helpful ally in the battle of syntax.

It is to my sandplay patients that I owe heartfelt appreciation for all they revealed so that I could understand how to interpret sandplays over the twenty years it has fascinated me. I thank them, too, for wanting me to write this book so that more persons might learn about this medium of healing.

To David Stonestreet, Psychology Editor at Routledge, and, to my colleague Andrew Samuels, the Jungian analyst, my grateful thanks for their real interest in my subject.

1

AT THE THRESHOLD

The lake of Zürich was covered in a fine morning mist as my first
analyst and I opened the gate of a Swiss farmhouse at the edge of a
Zürich suburb. I rang the ancient house bell. I recall noticing a date
inscribed over the front door. It was 1485. In a depression of my
own even heavier than the weather that day, my analyst Dr Violet
de Laszlo had brought me to the home of another analyst who had
an odd speciality. This lady, who opened the door and led us into
her lovely old Swiss farmhouse, actually had her adult patients play
in sandboxes!

With a kind of dread, I was eventually led down to a lower
ground floor room that looked almost like a barn. In it were two
sandboxes. Simple shelves, like bookcase shelves, lined the walls.
On these shelves were miniature toys and small objects representing the life objects that, in my depression, seemed heavy and grey.
They were actually, of course, bright and attractive. I thought to
myself, 'No. Never. These psychologists must be crazy. I don't
want to make constructions in a sandbox. How could that help me?'
I felt my pride as a person shaken in my lowered mood of
depression and despair.

I enjoyed meeting the analyst who used the sandplay however.
Dora Kalff was her name; she was a sensible-looking, older, plump,
quiet-spoken Swiss woman with eyes shining with enthusiasm.
Using few words in making conversation, she succeeded in
accepting me as I was – an exhausted, confused, depressed man
who might be referred to her for treatment as my present analyst
was leaving Switzerland for many months. In the nature of the
situation I became Kalff's analysand and eventually, after working in
verbal analysis for a few weeks, the moment came when it was
suggested I try a sandplay. Struggling to overcome my inner resist-

1

ances, I reluctantly entered the sandplay room and made the first sandplay with painstaking effort.

Much later, that sandplay was interpreted to me by Mrs Kalff as showing a positive diagnosis and many aspects of my possible future life path. I had projected my own future unwittingly during a state of midlife crisis and deep depression directly and concretely into the sandplay.

Twenty years on, I use sandplay as a part of my own Jungian analytic practice in London. My life has read out as my own sandplay suggested. I use sandplay because it does not let me down as a therapeutic tool with my patients. Its non-verbal images act as a psychological guideline to me as therapist in working with the constructions of patients; the sandplay experience for them is as vivid and often as meaningful over time as my own experience with Dora Kalff turned out to be.

What is the power of sandplay? Why is it suddenly in use much more than twenty years ago, mushrooming into a whole new generation of sandplay therapists worldwide? These therapists come from differing analytic schools and different clinical backgrounds. They come from the East and from the West. What are they embracing as therapists when they offer persons from every conceivable life situation an opportunity to make sandplays?

To begin to unravel the wonder of its therapy, I decided to write about my experience in using sandplay after the first decade of my professional practice. We are only at the dawn of an understanding of sandplay's therapeutic potentials. Two figures helped many others to witness that dawn of its use: Margaret Lowenfeld in her former London practice and Dora Kalff in her Zürich practice who, in addition, has travelled the world for thirty-five years to reveal sandplay's power to appreciative large public audiences and to professional colleagues.

The World Technique (Lowenfeld, reprinted 1979) was the basis from which Kalff departed to create a study of the process within a Jungian theoretical framework with adult patients as well as with children. Kalff had worked with C.G. Jung and with Emma Jung in her analytical training. An analyst pupil of Kalff, Estelle Weinrib of New York, has proposed several premises concerning sandplay therapy and its delayed, non-directional interpretation, in her book entitled *Images of the Self* (Weinrib 1983). She differentiates between psychological healing and the expansion of consciousness in the following ways in sandplay therapy: healing implies that there has been a wounding and possible impairment of natural organic functioning which has been remedied and restored. Expanded consciousness implies awareness of what one feels, thinks and does with a capacity to make choices in one's actions and communications that are relatively free of control by complexes. Healing in the context of sandplay therapy is a non-rational phenomenon taking place in what Kalff refers to as the 'preverbal level'. Two processes are occurring in the sandplay which can deepen and accelerate the therapeutic endeavour. While the verbal psychotherapy of Jung progresses (working with complexes, dreams and developmental problems), the added use of sandplay encourages a creative regression that enables healing through its delayed interpretation and a deliberate discouragement of rational thinking. The two processes complement one another creating a positive synergistic effect.

Sandplay gives the therapist a non-verbal image which may represent meanings within the therapeutic situation which are not known or not yet fully grasped by either the client or the therapist. Such images bring with them new psychological changes, substitutions, improvements, delegations, repressions and possible latent meanings in the patient's material. Mary Watkins, writing in the 1981 issue of *Spring* comments: 'As image and experience interpenetrate, the image is not discarded but becomes an eye through which one perceives and senses' (Watkins 1981, p. 117). The analyst's alertness and sensitivity to the power of image can enable the patient to interact with the sandplay and its structure, in order to see the symbolic in the projected unconscious content of the picture. Professor Jung believed that only what is oneself has the power to heal (Jung 1960, pp. 67–91).

Sandplay has evolved following H.G. Wells' book *Floor Games*, first published in 1911. Using pieces of wood, paper, plasticine and miniature people and animals, Wells and his two sons built cities and islands, and played protracted games in a room-sized sandbox. In my own childhood, in the late 1930s, I played in a sandpit 8 feet by 8 feet into which I walked, as into a room. It became my play context for a time, as it has become my 'text' of therapeutic play today.

In 1925, Margaret Lowenfeld left paediatrics to begin the psychiatric treatment of children in London. She collected small objects, toys, coloured sticks and shapes of paper, metal and clay, and kept them in what her young patients called 'The Wonder Box'.

These objects were moved later into a cabinet, the contents of which came to be called 'The World' by the children attending the clinic.

The children themselves created the spontaneous new technique of making world pictures in small sand trays. Thus Lowenfeld found a medium which is attractive to children and adults, and which gives both therapist and sandplayer a way to communicate and share interior experience interpretively. The elements of Lowenfeld's 'World Technique' have remained mostly unchanged since her early work in 1929. These elements are an imaginative activity with sand, used with or without objects, within a circum-scribed space (the sandbox itself) in the presence of a therapist.

Dora Kalff studied these techniques with Dr Lowenfeld in London in 1956. She then returned to Zürich to finish her training with Emma and Carl Jung. The Jungs sent their own children to do sandplay with Dora Kalff; Jung's interest in sandplay is not well known. As early as 1937, Jung interpreted one of Lowenfeld's sand-worlds at the Congress of Psychology in Copenhagen. In the USA, Eric Erikson used sandplay with young adults to develop his new empirical formulations about pre-adolescent play and about the psychoanalysis of women (Erikson 1951, 1964). Dora Kalff found that mothers of the children working with her in sand therapy became interested in sandplay for themselves (Kalff 1980). Men are now also extensively using sandplay therapy (Ryce-Menuhin 1984).

The suitability of a patient for sandplay has very little to do with age or gender: two basic aspects of the technique are that sand pictures can amplify and intensify the material of analysis and relate it to personal experience. This implies that it is very important to find out what the symbol in the sandplay may mean to the maker of the picture. In well-enough patients, sand-pictures have the effect of giving back a mirror-image to the patient and of enlarging his comprehension of himself. Whatever is happening and, even if the patient is unwell, sandplay is a tool of expression that can enable the patient to reveal aspects and subtleties of thought and feeling, intuition and sensation which both their speech and gesture may fail to present. The non-verbal feedback of just looking and intensely sharing the patient's sandplay has, in itself, a great power to clarify the situation for the therapist.

In the sand room itself, I provide two sandtrays: one with wet sand for modelling and one with dry sand to suit drier feeling moods. The sandtrays are half-filled with sand and have water-proof sea-blue linings which can be used to represent water. The boxes are designed to a size that can be seen without shifting the eye focus from side to side. The average size of sandtrays used by therapists in a recent survey seems to be about 18 inches deep, 23 inches across and 3½ inches high at the sides. I use a very slightly larger-sized box as the temenos or container; the size must act as a regulating and protecting factor for the patient's non-rational expression. This expression may touch a profound preverbal level of consciousness without any conscious use of regression.

As the world picture builds up – and most patients take from 20 to 40 minutes to complete a sandtray – there may be several stages of construction, including altering, or even destroying, parts of the picture. I record these developments by sketching them in my casebook, sitting quietly at a distance, and discuss these aspects afterwards, if appropriate to the patient's well-being. The sandplay is photographed after the patient leaves, and I never dismantle the sandplay in his presence.

These photographs are not shared as a whole series with the patients until either I decide it would be helpful to do so, or the termination of therapy occurs or a brief break within the analysis comes along when a review of the sand-work seems appropriate. I give the sandplayer copies of his slides only when the therapy is completed for whatever reason.

Assumptions about object-meanings is one of the controversial areas and the real dangers analysts face when interpreting sandplay. Unverified assumptions about creative ordering or the meaning of objects can be quickly corrected, if not quelled by patients themselves, who interpret their own picture as they wish. As my approach to sand-work is non-directional in atmosphere, the patient remains relatively unconscious about the symbolic meanings I may inwardly interpret, which gives sandplay its superb projective power. The patient continues to use sandplay during the therapy in a spontaneous, non-guarded way.

Lowenfeld writes interestingly about the importance of not assuming to know the client's meanings:

a world-maker, standing in front of an open drawer – containing a number of representations of houses of different shapes and sizes – took up a medium-sized house and put it on the flat sand in the world tray. To the individual who has taken up the house, it may represent "a house" but it may also, and with equal possibility, represent nothing of the sort.

It may be the nearest object he can find to stand for the idea of "safety", of "being under observation", of "the restrictions of urban life", of "family", or simply a conveniently sized and shaped rectangular object he can use as a plinth on which to put a horseman to form a statue.

(Lowenfeld 1979, p. 255)

And as to not interpreting too much, Dr Lowenfeld writes, 'The mere fact of making a series of worlds, and having them recorded, in itself brings about amelioration in the disturbances and discomforts of some children'. And, I would add, 'of some adults'.

The delimited space of the sandbox enables the player's fantasy both to be bounded and held within limits, and to go free. This free, but protected space is complementary to the protection and freedom offered by the latitude and the containment of the therapeutic situation itself. Within this free, but protected space, the important ingredient is the experience of the patient as he uses sandplay. The patient lives through the making of a world: the therapist experiences 'being there' alongside. Qualitatively, this 'living through' is not unlike what occurs in verbal therapeutic hours, only here the process stands by itself in objective form after the session. It is independent, within the patient, of any intellectual theory as to its nature, other than that it is a form of serious play involving creative imagination – with the holding presence of the analyst nearby.

From a Jungian standpoint, sandplay mirrors the Eternal Child playing archetypal games. Over time, this can bring into consciousness a new awareness of the child within and of the child archetype. Jung writes about the child archetype as an expression of psychic wholeness:

the "child" is all that is abandoned and exposed and at the same time divinely powerful; the insignificant, dubious beginning, and the triumphal end. The "eternal child" in man is an indescribable experience, an incongruity, a handicap, and a divine prerogative'.

(Jung 1959a, p. 179)

After Jung broke with Freud, he suffered a period of intense malaise: he decided to attempt to recover the creative life he had felt in his boyhood. His memories turned to playing with blocks in his tenth or eleventh year and he began a game of building houses, castles and whole villages on the lakeshore near his home in Küsnacht every noon and evening. So Jung and a form of sandplay have had a historical reality. Combining memories and dreams with childhood associations, Jung was led to the unfinished business of his childhood and to his own personal myth, which he felt he had lost to a certain extent, in following Freud even into sonship.

> The years when I was pursuing my inner images were the most important of my life ... the later details are only supplements and clarifications of the material that burst forth from the unconscious, and at first swamped me. It was the *prima materia* for a lifetime's work.
>
> (Jung 1961c, p. 199)

Fantasy, as specific and autonomous activity of the psyche, is, like every other vital process of the organism, perpetually creative. Jung writes about the four functions:

> There is no psychic function that, through fantasy, is not inextricably bound up with the other psychic functions ... [fantasy] is the mother of all possibilities where, like all psychological opposites, the inner and outer worlds are joined together in a living union. Fantasy it was and ever is which fashions the bridge between the irreconcilable claims of subject and object, introversion and extraversion. In fantasy alone both mechanisms unite.
>
> (Jung 1971, p. 52)

Through Jung's first building game in the sand, through active imagination, he set in motion an ongoing psychological process which he observed both in himself and in his patients. Jung writes: 'The creative activity of imagination frees man from his bondage to the "nothing-but" attitude and raises him to the stature of one who plays. As Schiller says, man is completely human only when he is at play' (Jung 1954b, p. 46).

2

THE ENTRANCE HALL

In my earlier book I have described play psychologically. Before moving into the nature of its specific use in sandplay therapy I would like to quote this background material to the psychology of play. It is important to grasp the idea of a wide-ranging, inherent *field of play* before coming onto its therapeutic uses.

Play is a universal element of childhood. Play is a concept on its own, not reducible to any one sociopsychological view of the universe or to any one stage of civilization. The play element has existed in all cultures and in all known historical periods. It may be described as a suprabiological form through which society expresses its interpretation of life and the world (Luria 1966).

Why is play civilizing? The play element introduces into civilization certain rules and the concept of fair play. This enables civilization to presuppose limitation and some mastery of the self, which gives people the ability to understand that personal conduct within any civilization must remain within certain freely accepted bounds.

A general characteristic of play is tension and uncertainty. 'Will we win? Will it come off?' are uncertainty conditions fulfilled in card games or football, in crosswords or archery, in shaking a rattle or reaching for one's toes. In the play world, if the rules are transgressed, the whole world collapses. In the same way, nations go to war if the currently accepted lawful rights of national sovereignty are overstepped.

Play has been considered both as a physiological phenomenon and as a psychological response. These approaches overlook an aspect of 'at-playness' in play that imparts meaning to action. The fun of playing is rarely measured when experimenters view play as quantitative. In some types of play, biological functions may be seen. A biological approach assumes that play must serve something which is not play. Theories about this mention the need for abreaction, for outlets of harmful impulses, for wish-fulfilment, and for a means to bolster the feeling of personal value. This may involve the release of extra energy through imitation, experimentation, assimilation, and competition.

The contrast between play and seriousness is a fluid one. Vygotsky (1962) thought that for the very young child serious play meant the child was not separating the imaginary situation from the real one. In this way aspects of play are irrational. A game can represent a contest, or it may become a contest for the best representation of something. Both Luria (1966) and Piaget (1951) agree that play is the leading source of development during preschool years.

In viewing play it is important to note how useful it is to early ego-strengthening. The child both pretends and tries to master adult situations through accommodation to external conditions and assimilation of experience into meaning. Play is an activity occurring before a behaviour is fully organized, suggesting that aspects of ego-development are underdeveloped. Play can be a preparation for life via the realization of the environment that it can demonstrate, as a repetition of experience and as the communication of symbolic fantasy. Symbolic play is assimilative in that it organizes thinking in terms of symbols and images already partly mastered. The child's egocentric position during symbolic play enables him to make a transition, over time, to a more and more accurate representation of reality. As the child is more adapted, play becomes constructive and eventually the child very gradually plays less by himself after he enters the arena of school life (Millar 1968).

The idea that play may be an antidote to understimulation or boredom suggests that the building of more ego-experience is needed within an optimal amount of stimulation. But the concept of optimal stimulation has a wide application, given the great variation in individual babies' metabolic and environmental stimulation levels. Both in its inner and outer reality for the child, play constantly challenges the ego through its directedness, concentration, and release of another

9

form of play or non-play activity. Play is very much the child's own private ego-directed world and is therefore a strong conglomerate, integrated around the ego very early. As the child grows, he learns through play's zone of proximal development: the imaginary is often near to the memory of the real, and voluntary intentions may combine with the formation of real-life plans and volitional motives. In creating imaginary situations, abstract thought develops. These abstractions, when expressed as rules, lead to the under-standing of rules and the later division between work and play at school age. Play is a preamble to work. In the young child there are many unrealizable tendencies and desires. Under age three, the infant wants immediate gratification. Play can be said to be invented at the point when the un-realizable tendencies appear in development. What interested the infant no longer interests the toddler. Piaget describes the transitional nature of play as an intermediary between the situational constraints of early childhood and play ideas free of an actual situation. In game rules, the child can set the rules by himself free of the one-sided influence of an adult or making rules he jointly establishes with his parents. Freely chosen game rules include both self-restraint and self-determination. The ego is being relativized and has a close developmental relationship to play for this reason.

(Ryce-Menuhin 1988, pp. 224–6)

Winnicott (1971), in describing an infant's first use of a favourite object such as a teddy bear as a transitional object, points out that the baby's first 'not-me' possession initiates the first deeply felt experience of play. Before this transition, babies use toys as if they were merged with mother and not perceived as separate objects, not even from the baby's body. When an infant first perceives mother as separate, then the transitional toy symbolizes the possibility of union between mother and child in their new state of separateness. This brings a quality of loving into the play area after earlier stereotyping of toys that represented only the body functioning of the baby or basic experiments to learn about the reality of environment. Now the infant is experiencing more than instinct gratification. The child begins to feel alive through the imaginative use of his separate experience and to place that into the psychological area of play. As a child builds up this play experience as a part of 'living' he or she is building up an area between 'me' extensions and 'not-me' extensions of experience. The infant is now functioning consciously, building up ego experience in relation to inner and outer contiguity with mother–father, family, and the general dynamic of playmates or others who may observe playing. Now the child begins to live creatively and feels his being connect with and into play objects.

From the depth of this experience, the root of sandplay therapy could be said to have been born. Patients come into therapy who need to rebuild confidence based on experience. This process is just what their childhood play did for them. They need to re-examine (or discover) how separation and independence could further help them. This needed separation from whatever psychological phenomena that could be said to be persecutory, or partly so, reminds one of that early time when in playing, a child first breaks away from what caretakers injected into the play area. Then a child finds an independent and free play activity.

Where trust has been broken between a patient (of any age) and his or her sense of life (both towards personal reality and the actual objective world) it is valuable to use the potential of a space of free play within a sandbox. This can bring into being a new transition towards individual creative living. The sandbox becomes the potential space between the personal and the general environment which originally was both joined to mother's love and eventually separated out from it, if trust and confidence from mother was good enough to enable this to be experienced.

How like this is to the image of the sandy shore, rising up from the maternal ocean and leading – as a transitional area – to the firm land beyond the shoreline. Sand and its use as the earth-medium in sandplay is important as *nature's transitional material* at the depths of the seabed, bordering onto the conscious landscape as it rises from the sea. A pathway of ego consciousness, based on further self-discovery, is what sandplay builds through its images constructed by the patient. Working with the sand, as if it is maternal-earth, has overtones of an early experience of the reliability of parental caring; where that did not occur, the therapist is used by the sandplayer as a hoped-for reliable person. The therapist's concern for the patient is not to make them dependent, but rather, the therapist must show or be able to maintain a quality of just being there alongside the sandbox experience; this engenders the feeling of being 'in the shoes' of the patient as well as accompanying his psychological journey for a certain time.

11

The therapist's giving of a security space, often in an unspoken way, can afford the sandplayer-patient an opportunity to move from therapeutic dependences toward autonomy. This can occur through the repeated process of building a series of sandplays which then are interpreted and valued both by the patient and by the therapist.

This joint interpretation brings both the 'me' and the 'not-me' into the work; the patient's ideas are 'me' and the therapist's ideas 'not-me' to the sandplayer; to the sandplay therapist, his or her ideas are 'me' and the patient's ideas 'not-me'. This gives a powerful set of transferences between therapist and patient at the time of interpretation (see Figure 2.1).

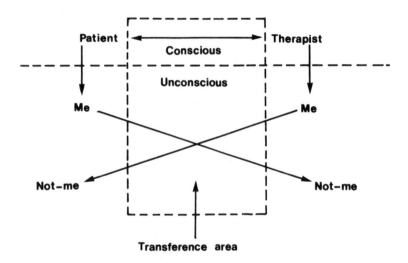

Figure 2.1 Area of shared interpretative dynamic
seen as central to the transferences within sandplay therapy.

It is helpful, within the power of this shared and transferred area of interpretation, that the original sandplay construction has been non-verbal. I remark on this because a patient can only use an analyst's interpretive ideas, if they are experienced as coming from 'outside' the patient and his own subjective phenomena. Because the sandplay construction is available in concrete, objective form for both the analyst and patient to see as *image*, words don't confuse (overlap, obscure, proceed tangentially, distort) the initial material – the sand-image *starts as non-verbal*. This means that the ambiguities of language are only added after the sand-image has been completed and this fact helps to evade some of the misunderstandings verbal therapy is always in danger of at the onset of its dialogue.

In sandplay therapy, the eye plays with the image, and then the ear may play with spoken interpretive dialogue between therapist and patient afterwards. This separates out the eye/ear confusion so inherent in image description in most persons. (It is known by professional musicians that the majority of a concert audience 'listen' with their eyes!)

Another important play factor in sandplay is the inherent free feeling one has (in ego terms) when in the serious spirit of play. Adults in sandplay recapture the imaginative spirit of free playfulness with its underlying intent towards self-expression. In creatively building a sand construction, an image is set out in a step-by-step fashion, without concern as to the 'maturity' level of its final appearance. This enables the dropping of many defences autonomously without concern as to *how* defences might be overcome. (In the verbal world such a state often leads to spontaneous humour.) In the non-verbal world of sandplay, experimentation in building environments for the objects used can be loose, easy, and free-wheeling. It is very simple to take out objects and substitute others. The relative quickness of building a scene in the sand enables very immediate use of associative ideas and images as the image changes during construction. The acceleration of achieving a desired image, however, still requires relative care in balancing the infinite possibilities opened up within the sandplay space. This avoids instant gratification, and the earliest regressions to the state of being a baby only very rarely occur.

The regression that does occur occurs in the play area or transitional area of the creative urge, so that by the time a sandplay is finished, most of the regressed elements may be re-expressed into the final form of the sandplay. This is itself a healing and integrating experience of 'parts' flowing into a 'whole'.

I believe it is the *non-purposive state* within which these part-regressions occur, that enables a working-through of earlier, unresolved psychic conflict and anxiety. This more relaxed, playful but concentrated state is not as quickly achieved as a rule in verbal therapies. Sandplay can sometimes lead to an immediate expression of problems *freed from verbal defences* which can hold up progress if not expressed early on in a therapy.

13

Where purpose is held onto very consciously by a patient, it builds the very anxiety that therapy wants to alleviate. Where lack of trust has been a potent negative force in a patient's life experience, the free quality of preverbal expression in sandplay – linking components without 'naming' them – can be restful compared with the challenge of trying to express in words the early defence–conflict situations. Often a sandplayer may unconsciously lay down objective–subjective 'scenes of childhood' in the sandbox immediately. These may reveal complex analytic material essential to the analyst's grasp of the situations within the case material. Non-sense and even chaos (see Ryce-Menuhin 1988, chapter 7) can be entrusted to the sandbox, when it might never be verbally entrusted to the analyst, or at least not for a very long time. A therapist should never impose order on this creative chaos but simply wait for further sandplays to begin to reveal, quietly and unconsciously, viable psychological patterns for possible interpretation.

The *physical and mental* activity that play involves can 'throw together' ego conflicts, forming a new sense of a *basis* for the self. The physical sense of play is very important in sandplay. One's hands relax into the feel and grasp of wet or dry sand and onto each object used in building up a scene. One may be touching, lifting, putting, moving objects of wood, clay, plaster, plastic, metal, stone, feather, rubber into sand and water which in itself can give a helpful, as opposed to an omnipotent, sense of mastery of a short-term loosely held goal: this goal is simply to finish the sandplay within the hour's session. This unhurried state helps the sandplayer into a quiet, relaxed play concentration, allowing borderline material to emerge and influence the construction. This releasing of defence through the physical ease of making sandplays, for which there is no technique needed as such, is of incomparable importance in relaxing a patient into a creative mode of expression. Only the most literate and literary patients could achieve a comparable verbal image with such free, unrestrained effort.

The picture-image built by the patient reflects back – in non-verbal objectivity – what the sandplayer can express in that one session. In this reflection can appear the summation of image-building communication for that hour which the therapist will receive as the self-material, within the on-going sandplay process for that stage of the sandplay. Depending on the therapist's evaluation of what is needed at that moment in the therapy, he or she may or may not bring words into the hour. A patient's creativity must never be impaired by the therapist's 'knowing' too much too soon. Patience is needed to allow the time and space for a patient to work onwards through the sandplay path, creating many sandplays on this journey. The fragility within the power of a sandplayer's expression should never be underestimated by a therapist. The psyche – naked – may need to be only observed at first, never interpreted irrevocably. I will quote from my earlier published work on archetypal theory. This discussion is difficult, but the reader will benefit from a comprehension of how Jungians think about and interpret archetypal images. Without this dimension of symbolic interpretation, I do not believe sandplay can be interpreted therapeutically in its most effective manner. Therefore it is of the greatest importance for a therapist's technique to include a very schooled and complete working knowledge of Jung's archetypal theory. In describing the nature of archetypal image it is important to remember that:

> As the subject and object of cognition are of the same nature in the science of psychology – that is, both are interpreted by one and the same psyche in a psychological manner and then also studied psychologically – it can be said that any or all psychologies must share this interpretive challenge. Jung came to the conclusion that beyond causal relations and manifestations in time and space within consciousness and the personal unconscious there must lie a transpsychic reality, or collective unconscious, where a relativization of time and space occurs. Physics has investigated the discontinuities in subatomic processes and has also, within modern science, been confronted with the problem of the relativity of time and space.
>
> Analytical psychology, formed on Jung's contribution and widely extended by others both before and since his death in 1961, is based principally on the study of the archetypes; Jungian psychology has an object to study and a method by which to study it. The object is the 'object psyche', which Jung originally referred to as the collective unconscious. This part of the unconscious is held to differ fundamentally from more personal material which has been repressed into the 'personal unconscious' because of incompatibility in terms of its acceptability from the conscious standpoint. The personal unconscious is what Freud emphasized in his model of the

unconscious. In the objective psyche or collective unconscious there is a second kind of material, expressing primordial collective forms that influence the way conscious material is experienced and which Jung compared to a crystal: 'The form of these archetypes is perhaps comparable to the axial system of a crystal which predetermines ... the crystalline formation in the saturated solution, without itself possessing a material existence. This existence first manifests itself in the way that ions and then the molecules arrange themselves ... The axial system determines ... merely the stereometric structure, not ... the concrete form of the individual crystal ... and just so the archetype possesses ... an invariable core of meaning that determines its manner of appearing always only in principle, never concretely.' (Jung 1939, p. 79) Jung views this unconscious material as fundamentally objective in the sense that its image in consciousness can be studied. When aspects of the collective unconscious become conscious, they can be discussed as elements of the objective psyche. Jung sees the psyche as just as suitable an object for scientific study as is the world of outer material fact. The archetypes or universal patterns of perception are contrasted in definition with the term "archetypal images", which means symbolic manifestations and the pictorial expression of the archetypes: 'These belong to the knowable realm of consciousness and occur as analogous motifs in myths, fairy tales, dreams, delusions, etc., at all times and in all parts of the world.' (Jaffe 1972, p. 51)

In 1936 Jung presented a paper at Bedford College, London (later published in 1959), in which he elaborated his view of the collective unconscious. The archetype *per se* is an unknowable factor in the collective unconscious which underlies archetypal images and contents and arranges them into typical images and groupings. Such a structuring element would be comparable to a 'pattern of behaviour' in biology which also underlies recurrently typical life situations such as birth, change, illness, love, or death. The phenomena of the collective unconscious are, unlike repressed material, transpersonal; unlike repressed contents which have once been conscious, they have never been conscious before but emerge as new to consciousness from the collective unconscious and are represented in images. 'The hypothesis of a collective unconscious is no more daring than to assume there are instincts.' (Jung 1959, p. 44) Instincts are likewise unconscious in functioning and transcend personal considerations.

The theory of the collective unconscious and its organs, the archetypes, is based on an assumption that the fundamental structure of the psyche is uniform. If we could eliminate the conscious, Jung believed, there would be little or no difference between one human being and another (in the original unconscious psychic content). So Jung has postulated an unknown 'x', a psychoid archetype in nature, unconscious and having a hypothetical vital principle directing the behaviour of organisms out of which consciousness grows. When it appears consciously it is an archetypal image which is seen to be the mental representative of instinct and which transposes the instinct into a conscious experience.

Mindful of the distinction between the personal and the collective unconscious, Jung criticized Freud's explanation of Leonardo da Vinci's picture *St Anne with Mary and the Christ Child*. This was based on the fact that Leonardo had two women who served as mother to him. Jung, in the paper entitled 'Dual mother' in *Symbols of Transformation* (1956), asserted that the dual mother theme is widespread, having motifs of rebirth, the dual descent or twice-born, in which the culture hero has a double birth, one human and one divine. Jung's examples in amplifying this idea include myths around Heracles, the Pharaohs, and Jesus: the rebirth ritual was used in medical healing at the dawn of civilization; it is found in mysticism and in infantile fantasy and is a central concept in medieval occult philosophy. Jung concluded: 'It is absolutely out of the question that all the individuals who believe in the dual descent have in reality always had (or experienced) two mothers ...' (Jung 1959b, p. 45–6) He also argued, using a neurosis where a patient appears to be deluded that he has two mothers, that the neurosis under review is not personal but a collective manifestation.

Jung began his formulation of archetypal theory in his work between 1908 and 1910 when he encountered in his patient unconscious contents which resisted integration into consciousness. This material was made evident in their dreams, symptoms, and fantasies. Jung was accustomed to receive from patients a projection of archaic motives onto himself as physician. These took the form of a transfer onto the doctor of the figure of the medicine man or magician. These primordial images – a designation Jung took from a letter (*circa* 1855) from Jacob Burckhardt to a student, Albert Brown, in which Faust and other 'genuine myths' were first described as 'primordial images' – were seen to have four regularly appearing qualities which Jung thought to be: repetition as a universal across races, constancy within the races, a fascinating effectiveness or numinosity setting archetypal images apart from other images, and regularity within each individual's life.

In Latin, 'arche' is the beginning or primary cause and 'type' is imprint. 'The religious point of view understands the imprint as the working of an imprinter; the scientific point of view understands it as a symbol of an unknown and incomprehensible content' (Jung 1969a, p. 17). Jung was not the first to be concerned with archetypal images. In the *Symposium* Plato described images, schemata, and inherited functional possibilities such as knowledge of universals that are supposed to be innate. In ethnology Adolf Bastian (1860) was the first to draw attention to the widespread occurrence of certain 'elementary' ideas. Hubert and Mauss (1898) called *a priori* thought-forms 'categories': 'They exist ordinarily as posits which govern consciousness, but are themselves unconscious.'

Jung thought it a mistake to suppose that the psyche of a newborn child is a *tabula rasa* or blank slate in the sense that there is absolutely nothing in it: 'In so far as a child is born with a differentiated brain that is predetermined by heredity and therefore not individualised, it meets sensory stimuli coming from outside itself not with general aptitudes, but with specific ones, and this necessarily results in a particular individual choice and pattern of appreciation,' (Jung 1959a, p. 60). Jung developed this idea when speaking of the 'child archetype': 'It is not the world as we know it that speaks out of his [the Australian aborigine's] unconscious, but the unknown world of the psyche, of which we know that it mirrors our empirical world in accordance with its own psychic assumptions. ... The archetype does not proceed from physical facts, it describes how the psyche experiences the physical fact ...' (Jung 1959a, p. 154).

Archetypes contain essentially mythological facts which have numerous centres, or nodal points. These essential groupings display themselves over and over again with the same ideas and functions. Some of the archetypes are the 'shadow', the 'wise old man', the 'earth mother', and the '*puer aeternus*'. They are best described metaphorically. The archetypes occur at ethnological level as myths, and their effect is strongest where consciousness is weakest and most restricted and where fantasy can overrun the facts of the outer world. '... this condition is undoubtedly present in the child ... the archetypal form of the divine syzygy (or conjunction of male and female) first covers up and assimilates the image of the real parents until, with increasing consciousness, the real figures of the parents are perceived – often to the child's disappointment.' (Jung 1959a, p. 67)

The psyche is seen as a self-reflecting system, the unconscious having compensatory capabilities to correct deficiencies in consciousness adaptation.

The technique of analytical psychology has been to find means to raise contents of the collective unconscious to consciousness and to interpret their meaning. The techniques of free association and dream analysis are too well-known to need amplification here. Active imagination, used by the Jungian school, needs more definition as it is not widely understood. If imagination runs free, a person may create a drama in which he plays a part, or a dance, or a vision. This can also be expressed through the media of clay modelling, sandplays, painting, carving, and drawing. Interpreting this material, which contains symbolic projections, necessitates its amplification by analogical method: Jung used the knowledge and viewpoint of antiquity to throw light upon the unconscious products of modern man. In a similar way the meanings of Egyptian manuscripts have been decoded by referring to archaeological finds of antiquity which occur in the symbolization of later language. Such insights and amplifications are used by Jungians to interpret symbols produced in dreams and fantasies. It is clear that Jung has expounded a theory of the unconscious and its interpretation totally different from that of Freud, who conceived of the unconscious as an infantile phenomenon. By infantile I mean that which belongs to a person's infant consciousness and is

19

developmentally limited to this psychological material. In an interesting analogy, Fordham (1944) points out that in physiology nobody would assume that because both man and child have a heart, it is an infantile organ. In tracing back adult fantasies to childlike roots, would the Freudians discard these experiences as merely infantile deposits?

It is here, with fantasy, that Freud and Jung and their 'schools' part company. Jung asserts that the whole of fantasy life is not infantile; parts of it are an attribute of man in general in the manner of Fordham's analogy: that the heart is an organ common to the human race at all ages. 'The unconscious bases of dreams and fantasies are only apparently infantile reminiscences. In reality we are concerned with primitive or archaic thought-forms, based on instinct, which naturally emerge more clearly in childhood than they do later.' (Jung 1956, pp. 28–9) These archaic thought-forms may contain personal factors, but impersonal motives may have great significance as well (McGuire 1974: see Jung's letter to Freud of 15 November 1909; 10 January 1910; 30 January 1910). Jung argued that there are ageless motives in myths, fairy tales and folklore, including ever-repeating themes which point to the existence of symbols common to all humanity. This led him to assume that there were impersonal nuclear processes in the unconscious psyche – he confirmed this on the basis of collective archaic patterns, the archetypes.

(Ryce-Menuhin 1988, pp. 25–8)

We need an 'as-if' quality to work with symbols; this enables an 'as-if' process to begin so that the symbolic attitude may build up on a person's sandplays. This symbolic attitude refers to a contact between the ego and inner psychic contents that in sandplay can lead to a healing process. This transformation can be brought by the ego towards the self in an approach which has the 'as-if' symbolic quality.

The 'transcendent function', a term coined by Jung, develops this contact between consciousness and unconsciousness through symbols; these symbols imply both content and function, both noun and verb, both actor and acted-upon. The analyst's job, according to Jung, is to mediate the symbolic function for the patient particularly through dream analysis and through the 'waking dreams' of sandplay analysis. The term 'transcendent function' here only means that this function helps a person 'transcend' or move through and across existing attitudes or a state in which they may be stuck (Bradway 1985). There is always the danger that symbolic material may be around in psyche, like a dusty unread book on the shelf, or that it may get acted out in a delusory, false, or exhibitionistic manner. This happens when the 'as-if' quality isn't utilized by a person. It is only when the big psychic systems within, such as the self, the ego, and the less-than-conscious shadow parts of the psyche, are more fully consolidated and present that the symbolic attitude can emerge and grow in the patient.

Where do we begin to learn to symbolize? Jung did not study early development at length and so it is appropriate to review the contribution of Winnicott here. You will remember I mentioned his theory of the 'transitional object' earlier in this chapter. Most children develop a strong attachment to a doll, a teddy bear, a certain blanket or object of clothing, etc. This is the first 'not-me and not-mother' creation. The favourite object becomes a way for the child to reconcile (or attempt to reconcile) reality and fantasy, the outer world and the inner world. The child works through the act of separating himself from others and, particularly, from mother. He or she gives up both omnipotence and mother/child unity and clings to the 'transitional object' for support. This is an imaginative support in which, for the first time, a child can allow 'illusion' to enter his or her psyche as a third area – neither the purely external world nor the purely internal one, but a third space. In this psychic space, play, inspiration, symbolization, and creativity can enter into conscious development. Later on the symbolic within man's collective expression in art, philosophy, mathematics, ethics, aesthetics, religion, cultural ceremonies, etc., can become more fully realized through the earlier development of imagination. Feeling for other people, in the sense of concern, develops as the ego becomes strong enough to bear separateness, self-reliance, and the boundaries of one's own being and of others' own beings. The self and the not-self must become unconfused before the true symbol-making can begin. Identification needs to give way to an 'as-if' representation of others: sameness and difference are then equally tolerable.

What we subjectively perceive and experience, or the archetypal content in consciousness, is different from that which subsists in itself. As the archetype *per se* is so deeply buried in the collective unconscious at its very bedrock level, we can never perceive it as such. It can be known only through its images in consciousness, e.g. as portrayed in sandplays. Our empirical knowledge is already caught and limited by this *a priori* structure of cognition.

When physicists researched into subatomic processes they learned that these processes defy (being both particles and wave forms) all set location in time and space. This means that the behaviour of an atomic particle cannot be observed independently of the process of observation itself. Observation alters the behaviour of the particles. In the same way an archetype is changed by becoming conscious and being perceived in its image as it takes its colour, atmosphere, or partial form from the individual consciousness in which it happens to appear. (No two sandtrays could ever have been exactly the same in history!) Between the conscious and the unconscious there is an *uncertainty relationship*. This occurs because the observer is inseparable from the observed. We cling to the psychic image as 'knowledge' but what the transcendental reality is, both inside and outside, is unknowable – yet it feels as psychologically certain as our own existence.

In discussing symbols we have to keep in mind these recurring subjective images that pervade the psyche. Whatever the objective reality behind appearances may be needs a deep reflection upon experience to imagine. This differentiation between appearance and reality is what the symbol may hold in balance within its essence. In symbology both the known or 'felt' essence and that part of its reality that is still unknown assume a part within a therapist's interpretation. Jung often remarked that he was quite conscious of moving in a world of images and that none of his reflections upon archetypal images could touch the essence of the unknowable.

We tend to think of symbolic images as meaningful when interpreting sandplay. It is important to remember that these images are also partly intangible to us, just as in language there is also the ever present duality of the symbolic containing a movement towards meaning; but linguistic intangibles linger on which remain beyond conscious meaning.

The symbol acts as a bridge; the bridging of what is familiar to that which is strange. It relates the conscious to the unconscious, the literal to the more abstract, the part to the whole. Symbols can relate reason to passion, the past to the present, the present to the future.

It is important to sandplay that the symbolic material be understood in a Jungian manner rather than in a Freudian context. This is because Freud regarded symbols as only the unconscious defence.

He thought that symbols are deployed by the ego to disguise the threatening aspect of memories, fantasies, or impulses. Freud thought symbols always represent the forbidden and that a symbol merely facilitates the displacement of a forbidden goal of ego-energy. Freud always seemed to be staggering guiltily out of the Garden of Eden having just tasted the apple.

Jung found these ideas much too limiting and much too negative. Jung always seemed to be enjoying the eating of the apple of consciousness. He argued that Freud was only discussing 'signs', not symbols, because the symbol was merely being considered as a substitute for a repressed object.

Jung saw the symbol, however, as a natural language of the unconscious and he wrote that symbols are thought to be the best possible expression with which to describe a relatively unknown and complex fact. Although the symbol is experienced as existing, it is not yet fully grasped by consciousness. The symbol is relatively unknown but this does not mean it is forever 'unknowable'. Rather it means that right now the facts, relationships and feeling experiences which the symbol conveys cannot yet be carried by less complex intellectual formulations.

In symbolization the form is connected to content: the physical configuration, the composition, the patterns, shapes, balances all connect to meaning. What is expressed cannot be grasped separately from the sensuous form that expresses the symbol. The content and the medium are indivisible.

I would now like to develop some ideas of the symbology of one object that might be found in a sandplay collection as an example. This will illustrate the kind of elaborative knowledge of symbols a therapist must have in sandplay work. Several years ago, Dora Kalff, the founder of the International Society for Sandplay Therapy, lectured in London for the Analytical Psychology Club at the Royal Society of Medicine. I had the pleasure of chairing that occasion and of having Mrs Kalff stay at our London flat. On that occasion she gave me a present for the sandplay; it was a white, double-headed snake in plaster of Paris with its coils painted a deep pure gold. The symbology of this universal oriental snake as 'meaning' can be built up mentally as follows: in general a snake of any kind belongs to the cold, moist element of water (as in the wet sandbox) broadly symbolized as the ocean, or, within Christianity as the Jordan river (the place of baptism). Snakes can refer to the instincts as prehuman, impersonal, and collective in aspect, symbolizing the lower soul of man. Snakes represent the feminine principle, hence they are said to be creative. They appear as the companions of the Earth Mother (such as Dora Kalff is to the International Society!). In Greek mythology Hecate, Persephone and Demeter are seen with snakes in their hands as companions and in Gnosticism snakes represent the initial, psycho-spiritual material (especially the brain stem and spinal cord as reflexive) which needs transformation from the primitive and cold-blooded reflex response to the differentiation of higher brain levels.

As masculine, the snake is a phallic symbol, so in its masculine/feminine androgyny it becomes a symbol for the unconscious itself. In de Vries's (1984) brilliant *Dictionary of Symbols and Imagery* he mentions how the snake expresses the sudden manifestation of the unconscious with its 'painful and dangerous intervention in our affairs thus being a manifestation of the unconscious mother-image'.

As archetypal image, the snake relates to deeply-rooted somatic and psychological processes; it relates to the involuntary nervous system which kicks up when a psychological problem has slipped out from the normal range of voluntary control. The resulting tremors and tics can be associated with multiple sclerosis, Parkinson's disease and cancer in humans. The snake's biological properties lead to mythical projections of three levels of being; it lives in water, trees or on land, hence the water is seen as the unconscious, the tree can symbolize the archetypes, and the land may refer to consciousness where the archetypal image can be experienced.

The venom of snakes contains both poison and an anti-poison which counteracts the poison's lethal effects. Hence on the old apothecary shop signs in Europe one sees two snakes coiling upwards. The snake's vibratory motion gives it pulse; its annual change of skin gives it a periodic nature.

Continuing its physiological associations, Kundalini is the 'coiled one' (shushuma) at the base of the spine which when 'awakened' through concentration and meditation, creates difficult physical symptoms like the shivers, shakes, and spasmodic vibrations connected to snakes' movement. The human spinal column has a serpentine bend in it.

Snakes also symbolize measures and boundaries or borders of the unconscious. Thor, the thunder god, wrestled with the serpent. The 'Serpent of Midgard' encircled the world. Both Kronos, as the Greek god of time, and Aion, as death, are often pictured as serpents. Symbolically snakes suggest a loosening of rigidity; they are the vibration within vegetative states as well. In Egypt, the snake coils up when it is to watch over graves.

Now I would like to 'zero-in' on the two-headed white snake with gold on its coiled parts that Dora Kalff gave me as a gift. First, the double aspect refers to two aspects of one archetype such as the poison/anti-poison and the in-time/out-of-time qualities all archetypes possess. In Persia two snakes symbolized linear time and Eternal time. The Indian subtle body has two snake-like conduits for the Kundalini to rise within. One conduit is for the Moon; it is white and refers to quiet energy and the involuntary nervous system. The other conduit is for the Sun; it is red and refers to passionate energy and the voluntary nervous system. It is interesting that my white double-headed snake has four big red eyes! I have mentioned that two snakes wind about a staff or a tree in the symbolic logos of the old European apothecary shops. The staff is Mercury's staff, the caduceus, related to the staff of Asklepios who was tutored by a snake and given healing potions by it. Mercury's staff harmonizes the two nervous systems and the right and left brain hemispheres (as the corpus callosum) or connecting 'pipe' of fibres connecting the two sides of the brain.

The ergodynamic system of sexual, creative and working instincts is harmonized and balanced with the endophylactic-tropic system of the restoration and maintenance of body organs. Snakes symbolize the tension between the autonomic and the voluntary nervous system. In breathing out one expresses autonomic or a sleeping state. If symbolically there is a battle between the two snakes, it would psychosomatically manifest in shallow or irregular breathing with problems in the voice of breath coordination (see Case 2 in Chapter 4).

In this duality, one senses the symbolic gates to the personal unconscious and also the gates to autonomic mindlessness, e.g. aspects of schizophrenia. The duality has an Eastern/Western reference in that the Eastern quieting of the mind through meditative techniques and control of the conscious mind which alters attitudes is not enough. The Western need, within its depth psychology, to 'cut the snake' at instinctive levels is even mentioned in an ancient Dhao text: 'The stillness in stillness is not the real stillness. Only when there is stillness in movement can the spiritual rhythm appear which pervades heaven and earth.' Being is more than what is left when you cut down the first snake.

Now for the whiteness of my gift-symbol given to me by Mrs Kalff: whiteness is a state of lowered consciousness, a quiet sleepiness in winter. In the Germanic pre-Christian legends, the white snakes gave kings knowledge and their near-white relatives were used by common soothsayers in the market place. Gopi Krishna (1972) has written that the meaning for the search for the white snake within the body (other than the white conduit in Indian belief, mentioned above) is related to a steady, cool and detached state of mind; hence in China the white snake symbolizes wisdom. Mircea Eliade (1958) claims that in final advanced Yogic practices, the white snake-effect, in its extreme limit, leads to a one-pointedness, a stasis in concentration. If *Samadhi* occurs, one experiences self as a spirit located only partly in body when one 'knows the cries of all creatures'. This is not a dream-like state but one of full consciousness.

Did Dora Kalff know what her gift could symbolize? Yes, for the Jungian sandplay therapists move about the world of symbols in their sandplay rooms as others move about the outer world seeing its objects. In Chapter 4 my cases will illustrate how symbology works within sandplay interpretation to bring a salutory therapeutic effect to patients.

In this chapter, I have indicated that *symbols are imbued with real life*. They hold a dynamic force containing values that are conceptual and emotional. Symbols are not just analogies or 'correspondences' to something else. Symbols offer the only possible way of accepting a reality of the world beyond that which history, science, or technology now offer. Symbols suggest the world is wide open and rich in meaning. They tend to grasp an overall organic pattern, a *multiplicity of unity*. (The double-headed white snake is coiled up in gold, a symbol of oneness, of Unus Mundus, of individuation within the multitudinous possibilities of personality – like Mercurius.) Because of the great depth at the level of the hidden roots of all systems of meanings, Eastern and Western, symbols seem to spring 'as-if' from one source – our collective unconscious. Symbolic activity in a whole people seems to be a *myth*, a kind of dream that contains this whole collective dream within it. The universal themes in the archetypes of Jung's analytical psychology, as expressed in the images of folklore, legend, superstition, cultural anthropology, astrology, comparative religion and the histories of art and civilization, all contain this quality of essential oneness. The unconscious of humans seems to move towards a constructive longing (as in sandplay) to 'make' symbols. The conscious mind moves with this tendency to imitating primary ideas of the forms of life, of its sacrifices, and its thoughts, making symbolic formulations of great cultural power – such as the image of the Christian cross.

The natural and the cultural duality (another two-headed snake) suggests that symbols transcend both aspects. *Symbols bind together the material and spiritual in the awareness of man* until the Earth itself can be seen as a symbolic object within God's universal 'sandplay'!

3

INTO THE RECEPTION
ROOM

We have now seen how the inner non-material world can be trans-
posed by sandplay into a concrete outer picture of psyche. This
transposition symbolically objectifies the inner archetypal content
through allowing it to have an outer material form. The intuition of
patients, which is related to an inward and non-rational impulse
involving the unconscious, may go free and self material can flow
into the sandplay unreservedly.

The process requires a sustaining ritual within the way the
sandplay room is used by patient and therapist. I want now to
discuss what seems to me to be important about this ritual.

First, let me define ritual as I mean it to be understood here. I
want to give ritual an anthropological emphasis of meaning. In
sandplay we are searching for an elucidation of the self of the
sandplayer, a gaining of self-knowledge. This can be thought of as
an *initiation* to a further self-realization. In searching for a word,
other than self, to express the wholeness of what sandplay ritual
might contain for a person, I found the word *ewekë* in the Lifou
language of Melanesia. *Ewekë* means the symbolic in man including
his thoughts, acts, actions, and discourse as they relate to his own
myth, his own being, his own selfhood.

In Maurice Leenhardt's book on the Melanesians he describes
ewekë:

> all that belongs to man is ewekë, his eloquence, the object he
> fashions, what he creates, what he possesses in his own right,
> his work, his speech, his goods, his garden, his wife, his
> psychic health, his sex. All this is symbolic ... the manifes-
> tation of the human ... This is an indication of the little
> differentiation established between being and thing ...'
>
> (Leenhardt 1947, pp. 172–3)

28

When one is initiated to a new relationship to self, one needs ritual to contain the powerful transformation of understanding involved. *One's being becomes sandplays for a certain ritual time of experiencing.* For this reason, sandplay needs a containing ritual which I want now to describe, which holds the *ewekë* (the totality) of one's experience of making sandplays.

For the atmospheric quality of ritual happenings to occur and recur in a progression, a special place of initiation is required. A sandplay room, separate from a verbal analytic consulting room is absolutely essential. The two mediums, non-verbal and verbal, deserve and need to have separate physical space for their ritual enactment.

Entering a sandplay room includes the colourful impression of the many usable objects on the shelves representing the world of psyche in material form. Curiously enough these stimulants to memory and imagination do not over-excite (except in very young children under five) even at first sight, because they represent a familiarity (visually) to the known world. I have often been asked if so many objects don't confuse the patient or make interpretation of sandplays too difficult. To the contrary, I am absolutely convinced that in all patients, except in the physically brain-damaged, the relatedness to a rich and varied material world of objects has normally been built up by age three-and-a-half so that the further stimulation of the unknown objects, which may also be included on the shelves, is a longed-for and needed completion of self-expression. This is as true for adults as it is true for children.

The choice of many objects is like a kaleidoscope of possibilities when we come to use material objects to construct psychological pictures. I completely disagree with those analysts who use only a few objects in play therapy. The arid, vapid and unnaturally empty atmosphere in representing the varied and rich inner world by only a few objects in play therapy is an anal, over-retentive illness on the part of these analysts. I believe it to be both ungenerous and sadistically withholding in atmosphere on the part of the reductive analytic schools who are so frightened of the self, itself, as the ultimate carrier of our self-expression. One cannot deny the self's role in the healing of traumatically wounded psyche. The self, through its *a priori* archetypal richness, is universally a multitudinous psychological entity even within the imaginative play of the most underprivileged, understimulated and damaged children – including the autistic child – who also welcome a varied and interesting world of sandplay objects with which to search for self-expression. You cannot 'reduce' an *a priori* archetypal heritage to only a handful of objects, even if in pathology a patient, at first, may not yet be able to make a complete or more 'knowing' use of the possibilities within a world of objects. Even in the regressive sense, the known changes in intrauterine life, which a baby experiences before birth, have so many differing qualities that to present less than a full panoply of symbolic play objects to a sandplayer is spiritually profoundly insulting to the nature of psyche. It is also inherently insulting to a patient. I repudiate completely the restricted environment of reductionism used by some Freudian and Kleinian play therapists offering only three to seven toys as a blasphemous, manipulative and sick representation of the given world in psyche. The psychological world of an Ethiopian child who is dying of starvation is fuller and richer by God-given outer and inner imaginative environment – in archetypal image alone – than that.

As a sandplayer of any age or background quietly peruses the shelves of objects (I use 1000 small objects) the objects 'speak back' to his or her psyche and are taken for use in building up the sandplay. I only loosely organize the general categories of objects and do not put them back in exactly the same place, but allow the shelves a free, slightly untidy look. This is a deliberate discouragement of the anal tendency to 'wipe everything clean', to forbid a free and mixed look to the shelves. So much in our average super-ego development, the ruling introjects of the authoritarian ego-layer within our psyche, needs the relief of the less than perfectly organized situation. However, I do keep objects, broadly speaking, in the same general location: 'humans' together, trees together, animals together, dwellings together, etc. This facilitates, but does not restrict, the patients' imaginative flow within the concentrated time of the actual sandplay creation.

I believe the *richesse* of the psyche demands these many objects as partial representations of our shared psychological world; they should be available for use if a patient wishes to use them. After all, a depressed patient will only see what he or she can, during the dark time when little energy is available to deal with the inner/outer world. During a clinical depression, a patient will sleep a great deal, to avoid the energy demands of the outer world which cannot be met by a depressed psyche. Once again, the sandplay room mirrors the real world and the depressed patient can mirror his or her inner situation by choosing no objects at all, if to do so would mis-represent psyche at that moment in time.

Twenty years ago when I worked through a depression of my own using sandplay, I made a dry sandtray during a series done with Dora Kalff. I could only smooth the sand until nothing ruffled the desert-like surface. Then my limited psychic energy was gone. Nothing was put into the tray. Mrs Kalff said this sandplay could have been made by a Tibetan lama who was staying in her house at the time. After making that sandplay, I returned to using objects again; in a few weeks' time, a two-year depression began to lift. The stasis-point, the moment of cessation in psychic energy had been revealed in the still sandplay and then it was o'ergrown.

Sandplay reveals the hidden tempo, the pace of psyche's development, whether in healing pathology or in following natural organic development. It is the mirror of psyche *par excellence*. What a pity to remain bound to words when such a powerful wordless medium can be a balancing factor in the reparative work of psychotherapy.

There is a sense in which this wordless ritual of the sandplay is a way, whether for men or women, to the feminine principle. In the universal sense of the feminine, sandplay shares the activity of accepting a conception and carrying knowledge to assimilate it while allowing a ripening to occur. This takes time and needs an allowance for submitting to something which is an unforced happening. No effort of will is required as the masculine tends to feel it a necessity to habitually draw from psyche. The feminine quality is an admixture of contemplation with attentiveness, a circumambulation involving the whole personality, the resonance of self, not just ego desires for comprehension as to more information or intellection. Sandplay experience shares much with this feminine mode; however, when the masculine is expressed in sandplay, it sharpens its definition precisely because it is seen against this feminine, unforced 'earthy' background. Masculinity can have a very full range of expression; its battlegrounds, its hero's journeys, its phallic pride, its colourful and creative mastery of space, its forceful power, its childlike omnipotence, its search for love, its demonic aggression, its genius and its love of God. All these aspects and many more emerge as men and boys delve into the feminine non-rational world of Eros and temporarily abandon in sandplay that Logos-filled, over-rational world of achievement men are so pushed into by most societies.

31

It is important that the therapist enhance the ritual of non-verbal therapy by a special form of 'concentrated' silence. I aid this by quietly sketching the sandplay's development, but never anticipating or unconsciously leading the patient, only following the sandplay with a sketch and a few notes to remember for eventual discussion. This 'holding' presence is different from verbal therapeutic presence. It is more detached, less free-floating in concentration, as the therapist is not immediately screening the image for meanings, as one screens verbal material, but is just being there patiently awaiting developments. A silent observing companion, by projection, may seem to be a 'knowing' one. Sandplay therapists still have much to learn and to know, however, because the state of the art and the science of sandplay interpretation is yet in its first sixty years. Patient and therapist discover together. This ritual reminds one that both priest (or minister) and lay person take communion within the same ritual in Christian communion – a shared attempt at revelation. This ritual sharing and being present together in only partly differing roles brings a democratic atmosphere to sandplay therapy that more reductive therapies deny. In the Freudian world, the analyst is in danger of playing 'God' much too much by constant use of regressive techniques in relation to the patient which lose the naturalness of the healing atmosphere.

The ritual of sandplay is of a place, a time, a world of real and symbolic objects which a person uses to make concrete visual representations of psyche while a trained therapist assists in holding the boundaries of this ritual by an experienced, witnessing presence. Joint interpretation of what happens is then shared in an interdependence by therapist and sandplayer when it is felt to be the right time. This may be experienced as session-by-session dialogue or delayed interpretive discussion may be deferred until the slides taken of a series of sandplays are shown all together revealing the developing line within the work.

There is usually a delayed emotional impact with which the sandplayer must contend during and after the sandplay hours. In adults the preverbal level requires deep energy to be brought forward and the stimulation of intuition and feeling is often exhausting to patients who rarely use these functions. The spacing of sandplay hours must be tailored to each individual patient's condition. This needs to be constantly reassessed as the series of sandplays grows. Patients of mine have worked from a rhythm of one sandplay per day to one sandplay at three-month intervals during a verbal analysis. The variation of effect is enormous.

My own preference is to use sandplay in conjunction with a long, deep verbal Jungian analysis of many years. However, I am deliberately presenting a clinical case in the next chapter of a mature French woman where sandplay was used without other deep analysis. In this example, I concur with Kalff that results from sandplay method alone can be deeply impressive. Of course in teaching and preparing sandplay therapists, I use the sandplay in its own right, as these clinicians have usually had extensive personal analysis before training with me in London. Often, too, analysts refer persons while analysing them who they feel could benefit from doing sandplay work as a parallel adjunct to their total analytic efforts. I have developed special personal techniques to avoid giving such a patient transference conflicts between the sandplay therapist and the verbal therapist. I welcome these varied methods of enabling psyche to heal itself, to unify its opposites within an effort to overcome the tendency of persons to have too one-sided a psychological development and attitude. All these different analytic methods need the world images of sandplay for their re-balancing analytic effects.

As symbolic play is an analogue to spontaneous active imagination of an ancient prehuman origin, its primordial quality (that of archetypal heritage shared by all persons) gives it a power to stimulate the regulatory function and hence the healing transcendent function of the psyche. Sandplay encourages a collaboration between conscious and unconscious fantasy images and the ego. Jung refers to this process as active imagination, and this is how he described it in adults:

> [A] dark impulse is the ultimate arbiter of the pattern, an unconscious a priori precipitates itself into plastic form, and one has no inkling that another person's consciousness is being guided by these same principles at the very point where one feels utterly exposed to the boundless subjective vagaries of chance. Over the whole procedure there seems to reign a dim foreknowledge not only of the pattern but of its meaning. Image and meaning are identical; and as the first takes shape, so the latter becomes clear. Actually, the pattern needs no interpretation: it portrays its own meaning. There are cases where I can let interpretation go as a therapeutic requirement.
>
> (Jung 1972, p. 402)

Any witness to the experiential happenings of sandplay might agree, but here I feel we need, as therapists, to exercise great caution. To let a patient go into life, after experiencing sandplay but not interpreting it, is rather like seeing that someone's broken ankle is mended (technically) but that when the cast is taken away, the wounded person is not helped to learn to walk again. In other words, I believe combining verbal interpretation and ongoing intimate work on remaining problems that one may have after the regulating self-work of sandplay is finished, can be important to a further therapy for the individual. The parameters of the self being infinite, it seems to me important that after a sandplay process is complete, a first deep spiral into and through self material (hence a discovery) has been lived through but that the stimulation this gives to further development can be something so enormous that we need to stay with patients further on in a continuing analytic endeavour. In my view, this has to be a Jungian analysis to correspond to the empirical facts of the structure and meaning of psyche as it actually is.

Who should come into sandplay therapy? This is a more difficult question than it may appear. I would not say that exactly the same persons suitable for verbal analysis should do sandplay therapy necessarily; however, many of my colleagues would disagree with a distinction of choice. As sandplay discourages the rational Logos-style mentality for its operative process, it potentially can help the highly specialized type, e.g. the Ph.D. graduate who is trained to doubt the non-rational. The irony is, of course, that most of these persons would reject sandplay as 'too infantile' or 'too unscientific', whatever strong empirical claims sandplay therapists now make for the healing properties of sandplay.

The borderline psychotic is rarely recommended for sandplay. Already in-built safeguards to warn a therapist of latent psychosis are contained in the insect and the whole reptilian world of play objects where a patient will discover a toy spider or an anaconda snake and 'flip' at once into the psychosis with very definite clinical, phobic features in a way that is not helpful to therapeutic process.

The control of words chosen by an analyst enables verbal treatment to be more clinically helpful over time to psychotics than sandplay usually is in my estimation; that is, in selected cases, I accept the latent psychotic for analytical work, but not for sandplay, at least as a beginning approach.

It is important for an adult patient that a certain degree of curiosity is aroused by sandplay if it is to be the suitable medium. In the case of patients over twenty, I prefer it if they themselves ask about sandplay, even including an expression of negative resistance, before suggesting it be tried. With patients under twenty, sandplay is usually a natural outflow of need, without much resistance appearing, as the nature of play is usually still present as a certain part of adolescent and earlier childhood.

When ritual is compulsive as in the obsessional, sandplay may be tried but it will rarely prove to be more than an added 'cul-de-sac' for the pathologically obsessive. It usually becomes another defensive ritual, to be added to the patient's repertoire of rituals, and although sandplay might reveal some projection from obsessional psyche that escapes words, this happens more often with children (including the autistic) than it does with adult obsessionals. They just tend to repeat their rituals, recycled into a sandplay mode of expression.

With adult hysteria, I have had some real success using sandplay. Usually the hysteric will have boundary problems psychologically; their behaviour will veer in several directions at once, in and through a broad spectrum of unrelated, various intensive behaviours, i.e. they may often be active sado-masochists, bisexuals, and exhibit 'Jekyll and Hyde' qualities. The holding quality of the sandbox, the sandplay space and the therapist's presence as ritual can help to radically challenge the hysteric into a focus of psychological acuity, usually after a series of chaotic sandplays with objects 'marching' out of the sandbox onto the surrounding tables, shelves, floor, walls or onto the body of the patient. There is a quietening of unboundaried impulse in sandplay, over time, which begins a curative process for hysterics that needs very careful tending by the therapist. Often hysterics are best treated in intensive short periods of sandplay followed by a cessation of three months, then again an intensive series of sandplays. This enables the gradual shut-down of unboundaried living-out behaviour during the periods away from therapy, as its cessation will require, like youth itself, to be grieved about and gradually let go. It is traumatic for hysterics to suddenly drop their behaviour patterns. This needs weaning both through sandplay and through its periodic absence. Verbal therapists tend to hang on too fiercely to hysterical patients. These patients need breathing space from any kind of analytical work and then its return in an on/off sequence.

Depressives can utilize sandplay most effectively if it is combined with deep verbal analysis over a long period. The intensity of wounding that lies behind a reactive and/or an endogenous depression should never be underestimated by therapists. The cessation of psychic energy available to behaviour has been pulled down into a depressive's unconscious and great patience (almost superhuman) is required by both patient and therapist during the 'dark night of the soul.' I usually suggest that a severely depressed patient make a sandplay only when they feel enough psychic energy may be available: this is usually in one out of four to six sessions, not more. The series of sandplays will carry the same overlapping characteristics of a series made one after the other within a shorter time, such as repeats of favourite objects used with new meanings and a progressive lay-out of self material; however, the depressive will need verbal orientation sessions in between the sandplays, to gain sufficient re-balancing to continue on within the black core of clinical depression.

In children the manic defence is usually so present that a depressed child can do a series of sandplays, at once-a-week intervals, and not run the risk of this becoming counter-productive, as can happen when adult depressives are 'pushed' too fast. Psyche has its cosmic, natural, inalienable rhythm; this needs careful respecting at all times in sandplay ritual. The ebb and flow of tidal psyche is cyclic in certain pathologies as, in nature, it follows the moon's periodic waxing and waning in appearance. Sandplay has a certain 'pull of gravity' that an experienced therapist can sense in each session with each patient. Sandplay is not a panacea or a cure-all. It is a sensitive projection screen, based on earth itself and the concrete three-dimensional perceived, objective world. From this objective, wholistic base a subjective expression is created by the patient, from conscious and less-than-conscious levels that may, when ritual proceeds to its higher levels, prove to be healing.

The sandplay therapist is not a priest/priestess or a guru. Rather, I would feel that a 'good-enough' sandplay therapist is a trained, professional psychological *companion* on an explorative journey of sand-image construction which the therapist witnesses in shared experiential being with the sandplayer. The therapist brings interpretation (where suitable) of the symbolic meaning, both one-pointed and in amplification where useful. This is given back to the patient, who, in being a sandplayer, may be re-connected to the child archetype and the archaic existential wisdom of other archetypal images which self chooses to let flow freely into sandplay. This experience may contain elements of awe and wonder associated with rebirth experiences in whatever medium. In this sense, it may sometimes be a wonder-filled or wonder-full therapy. Whatever self is discovered, the numinous is present as a gift of God. This numinosity must be contained by a professional sandplay therapist providing a ritual space in which the power of the sandplay experience can be safely protected at the very moment of its living enactment.

4

WORKING IN THE
SANDPLAY ROOM

The heart of the matter of sandplay is its demonstration clinically. In this chapter I've selected four contrasting cases showing different applications of sandplay therapy to very varied personalities.

The first case concerns an upper-middle-class man who came for therapy during his courtship and marriage to his wife. His integration of his batchelor-style earlier life towards the fuller responsibility of marriage and the changing relationship towards a stepdaughter and an expected child of his own was the main theme of the sandplay work.

The second case contrasts sharply with the first. Here a lower-middle-class batchelor struggles to free himself from a negative anima possession and through dream analysis and sandplay sorts out some of his problems before breaking off the work, believing Jung to be an infidel. This case has wide ramifications for male disturbances just prior to the midlife crisis of transition and has been treated at length for its pathology. Sandplay is an important release for the patient within this case material.

The third case is that of an upper-class French women who came to sandplay for one reason: to work through grief and mourning upon the death of her only sibling, an older sister. Commuting from Paris to London weekly, her work shows high concentration and an aesthetic nature being used to therapeutic advantage in sandplay. This sandplay has unique esoteric imagery within a successful psychological healing.

The fourth case is that of a 14-year-old girl awaiting her first menstrual period at the time her parents were divorcing. Using the synthetic method of interpretation of the symbols in her sandplays, a developmental interface was established with symbology illustrating the power of amplification and free expression in her gradual extraversion and entry into young womanhood.

1. THE STORY OF JOHN: A MAN MATURES IN TIME TO AVOID A MIDLIFE CRISIS

In describing the case of a 29-year-old man who came into therapy for a year, I am initially reminded of a Sufi aphorism which says: 'Fishes, asking what water was, went to a wise fish. He told them that it was all around them yet they still thought they were thirsty.' My patient, whom I shall call 'John', had youth, wealth, a happy new marriage, a top job, a fine stepdaughter and a wanted pregnancy in his young wife and yet the patient seemed 'thirsty' for life knowledge, emotionally insecure and unaware of his good fortune. He was of Scottish and Irish descent, a former amateur sportsman who had become a successful business executive. John had been educated privately from the age of eight outside of Europe and then, from the age of twelve, at an English public school. He had studied business administration and took his college degree in that subject.

There was a Celtic archetypal atmosphere around the patient's presence. He was overweight, tall and powerfully built but slightly sad in appearance. John had tried many therapies and tended to apply them immediately to group workshops he conducted for business executives. His motives in wanting a Jungian therapy were cloudy at first and his ego-defence was very high. This masked John's partly enfeebled self which was hidden behind an appearance of strength and determination.

Throughout this case, I had the feeling that I was working with a damaged but developed, almost heroic child in the man. Childhood traumata were worked through during the therapy but the feeling of the vulnerability of the 'hero' was always present. John tried to compensate for this inner, impotent child, by miraculous deeds in the business world.

The distinction between reality and the patient's inner world was blurred with Celtic boundarylessness. There was inability to make use of his frustrations and little tolerance for them himself. He showed evidence of reaction formation, almost exhibitionistic defences and repression. The very effective use he made of the sand, while positive to the therapy, also had an element in it of the concealment of his pain and the traumatic experience that lay behind it at first. During the work, the beginning of a maturing drive of the Self towards individuation could be seen initiated partly by the verbal and sand therapy and partly by a positive environmental influence in the patient's personal and working life.

Jung's four stages of psychotherapy and the sonata form

The process in the sand, in this particular case, can be described as allied to Jung's four steps of psychotherapy. The first of these four stages Jung designated as the *Confession*, the great outpouring of the mind and heart which can release hidden forces. It includes a catharsis of purification of the emotions through fear and compassion and was considered by Aristotle to be an effect of tragedy. The second stage is the *Elucidation*. The patient begins to need to remove libido from the therapist and re-invest it in his own personality structure. The third stage Jung called the *Education*, by which he meant that the basic values of both patient and therapist are more to the forefront in a dialectical confrontation. The transference and counter-transference must adjust to a greater degree of equality and direct interplay during this stage. The fourth stage is the *Transformation*. Here the integration of the anima and the shadow can set libido free to be more at the disposal of consciousness. This brings with it a danger to the patient of a mana possession and an effect of inflation. Amplifications from the analyst become appropriate as a holding element during this stage.

It is worthwhile to note that these four stages are paralleled in the four stages of the classical musical sonata form in the first movement – a fact which Jung overlooked. The exposition of the main themes in the sonata movement is a confession or a catharsis of the dominant musical thematic material. The eludication is represented by other following musical thematic ideas in following complementary statements hinting at a fuller working-out to come. The free development section of the sonata movement is paralleled by the education phase of the analysis where question and answer and discussion is extremely direct, and the final recapitulation of the musical themes in a more individual form, including new material and leading to a final cadence, is like the transformation with its individuating potential leading to the termination of analysis.

The sandplays

In the eight sandplays to be discussed, the pictures can be clearly grouped within Jung's four stages of therapy as they reveal the development process of the analysis (see Plates 1–8).

Plate	Therapeutic Stage
1	Confession
2,3,4	Elucidation
5	Education
6,7,8	Transformation

Sandplay 1

The first sandplay was made in the third month of analysis during the *Confession* stage. It shows the wedding ceremony (see Plate 1) six weeks in advance of the actual wedding of the patient. John said that the centre spire represents a religious place with a priest officiating in front, then the bride and groom, behind whom stands the mother of the groom. The patient's father, who died ten years earlier, stands alone as a white figure towards the lower right-hand corner of the sandbox. The patient thought the two great phallic sand towers to be like two hills in a mesa in Arizona, but due to their reappearance in several sandplays to come I believe them to be two phallic breast-nipples: the right one the animus symbol of the mother, the left one the animus symbol of the wife-to-be. John was putty in the hands of these animus-dominated women. The nuclear family, consisting of the mother, a younger brother and a younger sister, are shown on the right, according to John, as a black figure and two small trees among reptiles, with both the threatening and transforming possibilities that implies. John said, as he completed this picture, 'That feels fairly complete'. On the lower left, John and his wife-to-be are approaching from the deep unconscious in a boat representing John's dynamic self potentially with the inner hieros gamos as a possibility.

Sandplay 2

Later that month John entered the period of *Elucidation*. On the principal central spire, like the wall of a fortress, sleeps a golden child, as John's *puer aeternus*, which sits high on an animus-breast (see Plate 2). John said that the orange mock outer-space figure was himself and the purple mock outer-space figure was his wife. The Virgin Mary and Joseph, as well as a primitive ape and various trickster figures, represent a parade of positive and negative shadow figures the patient wishes to reveal and talk about. On the lower right the nuclear family area reveals a collective warring

41

group which the patient thought referred to the Iranian revolution and to divinely inspired cruelty between men. In the therapy, we continued to work through trauma concerning family memories which were dominated by the alcoholic problem John's father sustained until he died.

Sandplay 3

After John's wedding during the fifth month of analysis, we find his anima child (*puer aeturnus*) fused to his new wife's phallic breast (see Plate 3) and a frog of transformation on his mother's breast (right) which showed progress in separating out his mother complex on which work proceeded. The upper right-hand corner, the ego position, is empty. A great bear, the patient's shadow, still denies the ego a more conscious representation. The Virgin is now surrounded by children-as-angels. The patient's wife is pregnant and a stepdaughter has come with the patient's marriage.

The path of coloured marbles (lower left side) leads to the new fruit of his unconscious development. The frog can live above on the peak or below in the red trees of the lower right and left. The patient related to the frog with hope.

Sandplay 4

At the sixth month, John identified with his wife's pregnancy by building a path up to his Self-shrine, placed on a 'pregnant' mountain, no longer a phallic breast-nipple (see Plate 4). The patient remarked, 'I always miss the start of a path', so the Ego/Self is not well-integrated into consciousness yet.

The *ego breaks through* in the upper right with the support of the *Wise Old Man* and a very high, risky, jet-plane libido which is sharply phallic. On the lower left, the four horses may be the companions of dying and creating. We had been working on John's unlived grief for his father, who, in dying an alcoholic, had caused John shame.

The multi-coloured stone in the upper left corner John thought to be representative of his spiritual guest, which I related to his anima development.

The nuclear family in the lower right, expressed as trees, are – according to John – himself, his wife and his stepdaughter. They become important dynamic figures within the next sandplay.

42

Sandplay 5

At seven months the full-blown dialectical transference brought the *Education* stage of therapy, which I name, following the sonata form, the *Development*.

Here the three family members (see Plate 5) enter the wife's womb to visit the unborn child. The womb is similar to the 'mating' boat in Plate 1. The swans at the entrance suggest the elusiveness of the anima which hampers John's relationships which are still partly unconscious. The lower left brings transformative figures in the seahorse, the crocodile, the gorilla and the frog.

The ego, as a peace-keeping Knight, attempts to control the unconscious forces. This is the 'stiff upper lip' persona of the British patient. The patient saw himself in his child, by actually going into the womb in projection, and we worked through his fears about his wife's physical risk in pregnancy and about his own new responsibility both to his stepdaughter and to his unborn child. In the upper left-hand corner, the family totem pole and a flame of fire enhance this deep projection of the womb of the world, or of John's world.

Sandplay 6

In the eighth month the *Transformation* stage began. The shadow ape as John's shadow, is seen looking into a mirror which starts the transformation of the anima and the shadow within the analysis (see Plate 6). On the upper right, the house of marriage with the two space figures representing the primal scene, is upright. But three other houses are standing on end. This represents the difficult marriages in the family background.

John is entering a mana inflation. He sees the world as a 'many-breasted thing' and all of the nourishment can be his. The alternative elements, the white egg as his potential and his unborn child or the golden *puer aeturnus* can both be visited by the helicopter sitting on one of the breasts. The patient is inflated into a kind of would-be royal figure who drops in by helicopter to visit any projected part of his Self-Kingdom upon command. We worked through John's defensive egocentricity with only partial success at this stage.

Sandplay 7

Here a new ego emerges, the child of the Self, which is protected by conscious forces of libido, family and warring machines all on the

43

right side (see Plate 7). The *Shadow-Ego* Knight in yellow defends the birth of the true Self. The baby represents the resolution of opposites being fought over and shows the ego development as positive but as having been achieved at great cost. The opposing forces are formidable but they are backed by a coiled snake of Kundalini in the upper left corner. This suggests a powerful transformation is in action with a growth pattern.

Sandplay 8

At one year, this final picture was made (see Plate 8). John moved away from London for his work and the analysis was temporarily curtailed for this reason. John said that his own Self was represented by the robin redbreast on the boat and he felt full of feeling as he approached the shore of the 'Land of the Self'. Peacocks, representing the development of personality, greet the arrival together with an Oriental wise man and the anima as a Chinese sitting women in the ego-corner of the sandbox. But the great sea-urchin shell with its five-sided sea-urchin inside suggests that a partly faulted Self is being shown that still needs analytical help towards a further ego integration. This could help the Self to become a powerful fourfold, rather than a fivefold, structure and to secure its balance in a solid quaternity. The forces of transformation are powerfully shown in Plates 6, 7 and 8.

The four corners of the sandbox have revealed the four 'Devils' of this analytical case. The Chinese, when digging shafts in California gold-mines, never made four sharp corners but, with great effort, built rounded corners to the tunnels. This was because 'Devils come in at the corners'. The four corners, as represented in this study, are:

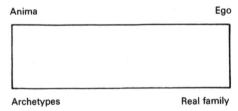

These four aspects remain the problematic of the case should this patient continue his analysis later on. The patient is at present still in the mood of the ego-demanding subject and plays mother to himself so as not to abandon the Self. He is generous because he wants to show how he ought to be treated with generosity. The therapeutic work managed to defuse and deflate the mana possession during the Transformation, but the work of building a stronger ego needs to continue. The true Self can only be mediated by a strong and developed ego. The ego should never be relativized back towards the Self until it has attained a maximal integrative and interpretive development within a patient's personality. This development may continue well into midlife and after until the ego may begin its individual relativization back towards and into the Self.

In the case I have presented it was not always possible for the patient to fully reach the symbolically presented development stages hinted at within the sandplays. Where a new order of energies was achieved by the patient, however, one can speak of his change within personal relationships as transformative growth.

2 THE STORY OF CLIVE: A YOUNG MAN IS HEALED OF TRAUMATIC CHILDHOOD EGO DAMAGE

Analysts often work with men from the upper classes. As I work with men of every background it seems valuable to present a case from my archives of a working-class man who had a difficult and inconclusive experience in analysis. However, he experienced a progressive sense of gradual self-discovering through the analytical process. In my recent book, *The Self in Early Childhood* (Ryce-Menuhin 1988), I have dealt at greater length with the introduction to ego development than I intend to do here. Now I want to introduce, for the layman and laywoman, the problem of ego damage in men during the first half of life to prepare the reader for the case study to follow.

This section is in three parts. It looks at ego damage in the first half of life starting with the birth of the ego in infancy. The clinical case reveals how ego damage can continue influencing development throughout the first half of life. In summing up I will consider the relationship of psychotherapy and religion within the damaged ego problematic.

The ego in theory

Most Jungians today would postulate a primary whole or integrated state at birth which is the unconscious self in its initial but un-differentiated totality. Consciousness can only arise if it is perceived through an ego-centre. 'Deintegration' is the term Michael Fordham proposed for a spontaneous division of self which enables the building up of the ego to occur. As a bit of the self 'deintegrates' out to the external world of objects, it tries to match to archetypal images projected from inside the self. Later the ego compares these images with its memory stores as they develop. Our memory recog-nizes, differentiates and recalls the internalized archetypal objects and ego-fragments as they reintegrate back into self and its ego-centre.

This process reminds one of the space walks of the astronauts who leave the total life-system of their spaceships, or their self-environment, and go out to collect any recognizable or useful bits of the outer environment. They then bring back this information into their ego-laboratory for investigation and possible assimilation. The astronauts deintegrate themselves, so to speak, from the self-space of their ship and go into the unknown outer space bringing back anything that matches sufficiently to their existing consciousness. This is measured by their technical ego-machines as, at the same time, their inner state is also being monitored. This material builds up into a knowledge centre about space in which their ego can pivot about weightlessly in ascertaining what has been discovered. Perception is not seen as just a passive act but as an object-seeking activity moving about in psychological space.

Deintegration by a baby, at first, is the state where he must find an object that exactly, or almost exactly, fits the inner image already archetypally present. The baby projects this image outwards to find a matching object. Only when this match is reintegrated back into the new and growing ego can perception occur in the first weeks of life. There is rough agreement between Piaget and Jung on this point. Piaget postulates an inherited schema already present in the child's psyche to which outer objects must relate for perception to happen. Jung goes further and says this global scheme of primal inner requirements in the baby is the archetypal world of the collec-tive unconscious. This is like a many-faceted kaleidoscope of psychological traits collected from man's entire history.

As it develops, the ego becomes a great processing centre

running twenty-four hours a day at differing intensities. It must handle all of the impinging input to consciousness whether from outside the body or from inside it. Freud discovered a repression system which can make incoming contents inoperative, and which can be resorted to when the input threatens the new and weak ego of the baby. The ego adapts to the reception or the exclusion of stimuli depending upon the considerations of self-preservation of the ego as maintained by the repression system. According to Freud, 'repression is not a defence mechanism present from the very beginning ... it cannot occur until a sharp distinction has been established between what is conscious and what is unconscious' (Freud 1925).

The immature ego of the child is particularly vulnerable to both internal and external dangers. It defends itself against over-whelming demands of the internal input such as threatening instinctual contents from the collective unconscious. The child's ego is vulnerable to external dangers because, although the parents may ideally create a security for their baby's ego, the baby pays for this security by fearing he may lose the love of his caretakers. This could render him helpless to many dangers of the outer world. Repression of these security fears as well as internalization of the primitive threats from parents influence the repression sequence. Every culture moulds parents' opinions as to what behaviour in the child should be punished. Punishable ideas, or memories relating to ideas that are punished, would be what Freud considered unpleasant content that might be repressed.

Another example of the ways in which parents influence ego development both positively and negatively can be found in the concept of the ego-ideal. The infant's identification with its long period of helplessness and dependence upon the parents creates an internalization of this influence as an ego-ideal. Normally this begins with the mother and her nutritive role but the masculine side of early influence is further developed now that many fathers are tending to take a more active role with babies from their birth. It is fair to caution fathers, however, that their nurturance of the baby may not be good enough for the initial needs within the caretaking as experienced by the baby and that men's desire to undertake this task may involve their own paternal psychopathology. Whatever the parenting contains, Freud has reminded us that the ego-ideal gives a 'permanent expression of the influence of the parents' onto the child (Freud 1927). This absorption of influence by the ego-ideal spreads to include siblings, relatives and close friends of the household. Jung maintained that the real mother evokes the mother archetype in the psychic structure of the child and that this can function independently of the mother's reality, as a compensating pyschic fact. The same would be true of the instigation of the father type. Jung writes:

> The danger is just this unconscious identity with the archetype: not only does it exert a dominating influence in the child by suggestion, it also causes the same unconsciousness in the child, so that it succumbs to the influences from outside and at the same time cannot oppose it from within. The more a father identifies with the archetype, the more unconscious and irresponsible, indeed psychotic, both he and his child will be.
>
> (Jung 1961b, p. 316)

To prevent this, both parents need a strong identification with their child so that the frustrations of reality will only be experienced by the baby in a strength, and, at the time his developing ego can actually manage to cope.

Whatever the parenting, the ego-ideal is inferred from the mother and father or their substitutes and influences the development between the infant and other individuals. This influence has a hierarchical, conservative and authoritative tendency within the ego. It is experienced within the ego. It is experienced by the infant throughout the discipline and learned strictures of behaviour from the parents or caretakers. This influence of the ego-ideal continues to operate, with modification, throughout life. Jung comments:

> Generally speaking, all the life which the parents could have lived but of which they thwarted themselves for artificial motives is passed on to the children in substitute form. That is to say, the children are driven unconsciously in a direction that is intended to compensate for everything that was unfulfilled in the lives of their parents.
>
> (Jung 1954a, p. 191)

As the original unity of the self gets split up into growing islands of ego-consciousness, the child begins to say 'I' and the early ego-personality begins to ask 'Why?'. With this question 'Why?', the ego begins another stage of adaptation to new and unknown conditions which is the purely cognitive quest – the wanting to know. This is not just knowing the biologic condition of the self and its defences – about which Anna Freud, Michael Fordham, Otto Kernberg, Heinz Kohut, and Leopold Stein have told us much – but the start of a discrimination within the ego's possibilities to separate and sort out and classify its cultural environment, as Winnicott has brought to our attention. The child begins to use the ego to wonder both about the cause and the effect of events and what their purpose might be. This leads on eventually to the concern with possible meanings in our life and our relation to the creating energy of the universe as a whole or to God as the supreme life-force.

Jungians believe that this developing ego-consciousness has its depth of psychological being in the mythical images of the collective unconscious. Gerhard Adler writes:

> The great collective images of the past are still so near and powerful in the case of a child that his first task is to free himself from the fascination of their super-personal power, and in conflict with these forces he must forge his own small personality, thus extricating and developing his still very fragmentary individual ego. This decisive development away from a state of identification with collective psychic contents into a sharply individual ego which has to experience and recreate the inner and outer realities, the whole of the world, psychologically speaking, would be non-existent.
>
> (Adler 1966)

There is thus a tremendous tension between our original natural condition and that of a mature ego-consciousness.

The ego is brought into danger during its development in several ways. First, ego damage may occur if the parental archetypes which are projected on the real parents have to be withdrawn because of the ego's realization that the imperfections and failures of the actual parents don't match the archetypal image.

Second, splitting may occur if the ego-ideal operates onto the total ego with undiminished primal force. The more the existentially related ego-centre grasps that the established images of the parents were not the reality, the more it tries to withdraw and split off from the ego-ideal's pressures. Often the ego regresses when it needs an earlier level of integration to escape this split and to start again from an ego-unit or its initial infantile wholeness of self.

Third, where the parents were largely unavailable as mothers and fathers, the ego may need a narcissistic mirror-image to hold it from disintegration. For such children, a father's anger may make the child believe in a vengeful and punitive God, Yahweh, casting them into the wilderness. Where the mother's capacity to respond to her infant by being a mirror to him is not good enough, the child may fail to develop a healthy experience of himself so that 'I' can become 'me'. Pathological levels of damage to the parents' image in the child's psyche lead to an intense alienation and enfeebled self. This includes the resultant sense of envy and hatred of others whom he considers more fortunate than himself.

Fourth, the ego's problems are by no means over when it succeeds in starting to integrate the unconscious contents into the existing ego-personality. This process can lead to various psychopathologies: neurotic dissociations, schizophrenic fragmentation or, in the extreme, ego dissolution with a blind take-over of contagious preconscious ideas. If the ego structure is strong enough to withstand the pressure of the assimilation of unconscious contents, someone who has an overly ego-centric will may feel paralysed by the new vitalization of the self's personality. This can act as a compensatory function to ego-consciousness itself. Inflation and a mana personality may result.

When the damaged or weak ego is not psychologically repaired, the ongoing result is well illustrated by the clinical case I want to share. This case history speaks for itself as an example of how ego damage can thwart normal development throughout the first half of life. It will be helpful to consider dream material, sexual facts and the role of religion in psychotherapy within this real-life sample of ego damage.

We are ready to consider the question: 'Whatever happened to this analysand's ego?'

Ego in a clinical case

The facts, but not the ideation, have been totally altered in this case presentation so that any resemblance to persons living or dead is purely coincidental. The analysand, whom I shall refer to in alias as 'Clive', has given me permission to publish this case in this form for which I am grateful.

Clive presented a narcissistic character disorder involving unconscious bitterness over his origins and early life experience, a compulsive and unhappy sexual pattern and great ambivalence towards his birthplace, Cornwall. Clive began therapy with me in his early thirties. He described himself as an out-of-work actor and was employed as a clerk in a factory. Upon entering analysis, Clive wanted help in understanding his dreams. He had recently had a recurrent dream which made him fearful of being self-destructive.

Clive was the firstborn of several children. His father had mostly worked abroad and had been away throughout Clive's early boyhood. Traumatic experiences during World War II caused the father repeated illnesses when he returned home. Shortly before Clive was born his mother contracted severe pneumonia and was hospitalized and put on the critical list. Mother and child were in labour three days and Clive was born only half-conscious and choking. He contracted whooping cough during his second week in the special-care unit and was separated from his mother for several weeks. He was nursed by a Cornish wet-nurse. Still today Clive is always afraid of lung disease and his voice is a problem to him in acting. He tends to feel panic in his vocal chords and oppression in his chest.

In the years following his birth, several children were born to the family. As Clive's father was chronically ill, his mother commuted daily to a nearby town for work. For a decade Clive was principally raised by a severe, animus-ridden cousin. She inflicted regular punishment upon Clive by making him dress in girls' clothing for a day and endure the chides of his younger siblings and the neighbours. Clive describes his cousin as 'tough, devouring, brazen, evil, matriarchal and monstrous'. Dressing in women's clothing in no way shook the boy's heterosexual future in general, but, in particular, it made Clive wary of a woman's authoritative tendencies be they controlling or influencing. He used his imagination reck-lessly and his fantasies and visions were powerful. He wanted to become an actor to escape his household, especially as his father kept insisting he should become an accountant or a solicitor. He was unsuited for these tasks. I quote from D.H. Lawrence (1922): 'Let us beware and beware and beware of having a high ideal for ourselves. But particularly let us beware of having a high ideal for our children. So doing, we damn them.'

Clive did not finish college or acting school but he did manage to join a small theatre company and play in the provinces. He eventu-ally drifted to the Eastern bloc and had a passing affair with the daughter of a friend. He returned to a city in the Midlands and made a local girl pregnant whom he then married, a marriage that lasted eighteen months. Clive converted to the girl's religion at that time, having tried several faiths. A healthy son was born to the couple but Clive's wife had radical political connections which frightened Clive away. Coming to the south of England, he found clerical work, which he hated and which didn't pay enough for him to keep up with alimony payments or his son's partial support. Neither before nor after his eventual divorce would Clive fully acknowledge responsibility towards his son. He defaulted on his upkeep payments with minimal apparent concern.

The therapy began with my awareness that Clive had never known the feeling of experiencing a relationship. He presented as a neurotic, narcissistic personality, an intuitive feeling type with moderate depression. This depression was held back in the sessions behind a bright, if false, persona. His persona had some wit and charm and theatrical sophistication.

With his mother and father so sadly absent as good-enough parents during Clive's infancy, I was confronted with a severely damaged ego trying to defend against a mostly absent mother, a negative father and a fear of the witch-bitch cousin. This ego damage led to several primitive agonies that develop when parents or caretakers have not supplied an auxiliary ego-function during the time of a baby's absolute dependence. Winnicott (1974) lists samples of these agonies, the following of which Clive exhibited:

A   Falling for ever. (Defence: self-holding.)
B   Loss of psychosomatic collusion, failure of indwelling. (Defence: depersonalization.)
C   Loss of sense of real. (Defence: exploitation of primary narcissism.)

At comprehensive school Clive had been kicked out at sixteen because of sexual exhibitionism. Behind this, I learned of a relationship to his penis that made one think he used his sexual organ as a transitional object, or a part-self object, in an effort to gain the autonomy which was missing in his weak and damaged ego. His penis represented an early 'not-mother' object but later, unfortunately, also seemed to be a 'not-me' object as well. This led to separating the penile erection from the whole person in sexual image (e.g. masturbatory). Normally an orgasm can 'throw together' and reconsolidate boundaries in the self, but for Clive compulsive masturbation kept him in a boundary-less phallic fantasy, robbing him of those very qualities of an erect, virile and creative person-ality that less compulsive sexuality might enhance. Clive became promiscuous with women in his middle twenties and found he could delay or even refrain from orgasm during very prolonged intercourse. I see this as his inability to feel relationship and to commit or even share his orgasm psychosomatically.

It can be seen in this case that self-holding and the loss of psychosomatic collusion (using Winnicott's language) leads to the defence of depersonalization in sexual life. At the extreme, Clive's sexual detachment became sadistic. He could pick up women he found very ugly deliberately to seduce them once and never see them again. He usually chose women for sex, however, who were attractive and who had money which he could 'borrow' to pay debts and to loan to a favourite mistress of the moment. His persona through all of this was always basically the same: bright, pleasant, humour-filled, off-hand and almost innocent. His persona was split off from his actual actions, but it held up from his own point of view as many people took him at face value.

With these narcissistic sexual problems in mind I want to look at specific dream material which illustrates developments upon other themes in the analysis. The dreams, in order of appearance, will include:

1 Inflation of the anima
2 The depressive, weak ego
3 The birth trauma reparation
4 The shadow.

The dreams were vital to interpretation as little changed externally in Clive's life during the first year of therapeutic work. He moved house once, moved mistresses twice and never moved sessions, always arriving on time. For the first ten months he continued to work as a clerk.

Dream number 1

The first dream Clive brought in was described as follows:

A leading woman TV newscaster from BBC 1 was standing in a deserted television soundstage. She began climbing the ladders up above the stage until she was near the roof. She called out, 'It's all too high, it's dangerous'. A man appeared who was her TV producer and, dripping with malice, said, 'It's all right, love'. The woman fell off to her death.

We may say that Clive's anima, as an actor, is represented by the female star of newscasting. In popular terms, TV sets are known as 'the box'. The box is a feminine symbol which can refer to the unconsciousness anima. TV is rather like Pandora's box in the sense of its unexpected, excessive and destructive potentialities. The anima climbs the high ladder of TV success in a kind of imaginative exultation. The producer, representing authoritative exploitation in general, sadistically leads the anima on to its death fall. Clive associated to his hatred of theatrical producers, his longing for TV work and his jealousy of successful TV personalities from an attitude revealing an anima inflation. We can liken the fall in the dream to man's Fall: 'Man died ... because his inner desires bursting out from the inner fiery centre ... tended towards external and temporary birth' (J. Böehme 1682).

Clive never worked at his acting; he did not perfect his voice, learn roles off-stage or try to direct. He wanted cheap and vaulted success on television as a reflection of an inflated anima. The TV woman, personally unknown but collectively known as a celebrity, becomes the beloved siren, who leads Clive's anima away from reality by enchantment and enticement.

Clive's reaction to the dream was revealing. He neither coldly detached himself from its horror, in the manner of borderline narcissistic cases (of which he was not one), nor did he react with much feeling to the woman's deathfall in the dreams. Diagnostically this suggested his negative narcissism was not at pathological level. Instead it had to do with a defensive and highly neuroticized set of complexes involving his early family history. This led him to problems in connecting with the issues the unconscious brought forward in his dreams.

Dream number 2

At the same time Clive was moderately depressive and a dream set upon Bodmin Moor suggests the beginning of understanding and growth based on a knowledge of the opposites. The dream reveals Clive's weak ego but it also hints there may be a possibility to grasp some self-knowledge potentially. Clive described this dream in session 20 as follows:

I am standing upon a wintry Bodmin Moor. I am peering ahead to determine if it is snowing. Yes, it is; the hills are

Plate 1

Plate 2

Plate 3

Plate 4

Plate 5

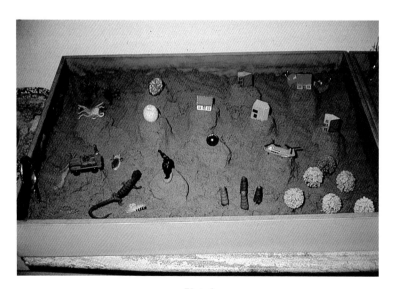

Plate 6

Plate 7

Plate 8

Plate 9

Plate 10

Plate 11

Plate 12

Plate 13

Plate 14

Plate 15

Plate 16

Plate 17

Plate 18

Plate 19

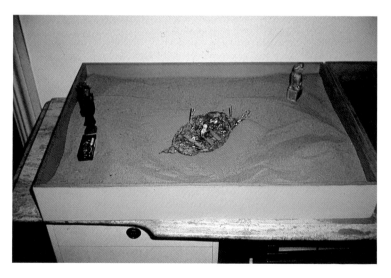

Plate 20

Plate 21

Plate 22

Plate 23

Plate 24

Plate 25

Plate 26

Plate 27

Plate 28

Plate 29

Plate 30

Plate 31

Plate 32

Plate 33

whitening. The Duke of Edinburgh appears. I greet him and we speak together, I tell him that I want to write. The Duke answers, 'Writing allows you to enter the inside of life'. The Duke walks ahead and scales a high hill. We discuss Christ and Moral Rearmament together. The Duke asks, 'What do you have against Moral Rearmament?' I answer, 'I feel it's wrong but I don't know why'.

Here we see two men at opposite ends of a social spectrum: a working-class Cornish actor and the father of the Duke of Cornwall. To offset this difference, Clive claims he can write and the Duke admits Clive might get inside of life that way. Royals, to a certain extent, are always partly held outside normal life in the countries they represent, except in their ceremonial capacity when they carry all of society symbolically. The discussion about Christ and Moral Rearmament suggests the self and how to place the self into spiritual movements as an ongoing problem. This may not be only one of Clive's problems but a collective problem that men everywhere might talk about. Bodmin Moor, for Clive, is covered with a chill; the white snow hides the green tundra symbolizing Clive's alienation from his beginnings. He has searched in other countries to find identity. He has nothing to say to the Duke of Edinburgh about Cornwall. The whitening of the hills also suggests albedo, or the first transmutation to quicksilver, in the alchemical process. There is some sense, too, to conjunction between the male principle, represented by the Duke, and the unconscious feminine, represented by the motherland of Cornwall and the Muses of writing. These Muses, such as Calliope, Erato and Thalia frequented Mount Olympus and hence could lead to an inflated anima. The symbolic inner union of male and female principles, represented in myth by the union between Apollo and certain of the Muses, would be one of the goals for the entire analysis.

The ease with which the Duke scales a high hill may refer to an inner loftiness of spirit, and, in alchemy, it would suggest a hollow mountain in which the 'philosopher's oven' is contained. The white mountain may also refer to the fixed position of the pole star linked to the polar mountain which bears the symbolism of the world-axis. When I asked Clive why he didn't like Moral Rearmament, he replied, 'Oh, they are all from the upper class'. Clive's depression hovered about his frustrations concerning his class background and his inability to secure an adequate foothold in general society. His narcissism, of course, constantly worked against this as well.

This was only the third month of analysis and I did not interpret very much to Clive. Clive was able to talk about his ambivalence to growing up in Cornwall which was a relieving element to his catharsis at the time. With care, it also seemed suitable to confirm to Clive that he did have some depression behind his quite cheerful persona. It was a free-floating depression which often blocked his memory of real life.

Dream number 3

The next dream was valuable because it helped the repair and reparation of Clive's severe birth trauma. Clive described this dream in the 34th session in a pained and hushed voice:

> There is a huge stone vagina. It has scorch marks on its internal sides and I hear animal sound of suffering. I am feeling terrible pain. A tiny infant is born burnt to charcoal. An angel appears, saying, 'I am light.' She holds and bathes the child with oils. There is an anaconda snake just waiting nearby, a blessed snake that is praying. As the snake opens its mouth waters gush out. The waters are silken and healing waters and they are washed back up through the vagina.

The horrors of Clive's three days in labour are contrasted here with the healing powers of the unconscious. The anaconda is a snake that likes both water and land. It is a symbolic unifier of conscious and unconscious and has the power to transform the birth canal into a place of silken moisture.

This is also a reference to the penis and its power to influence vaginal fluids. The angel may represent the unknown wet-nurse who bathed and fed Clive for the first weeks of his life. If so, it suggests that Clive managed to contain massive anxieties when his mother was separated from him by 'worshipping' the healing manifestation of the unknown woman from another dimension, the wet-nurse 'angel'. The waters gushing from the anaconda suggest the maternal, the preserver of life circulating in rain, sap, milk and blood. Water symbolism concerns the struggle of the psyche to formulate a clear message for the conscious mind. The struggle of Clive's actual birth was reconstellated in the dream and partly healed through the symbolic waters from the anaconda. This aids the *solutio* and *distillatio* in the alchemical process.

There was a sense in which Clive's transference to me deepened at this time: he had never trusted anyone or finished any project he undertook and the next period of the analysis was developmental. He was more present and seemed partly changed. His personal character did not change but his grasp of verbal associations was clearer and freer. He was more relaxed and brought more of himself into the sessions.

Dream number 4

In a dream from session 37 Clive's alter-ego appears: in the dream Clive is followed by a man who looks like him onto a tube train. Clive tries to escape his look-alike by saying he is going 'in the wrong direction'. The next station is the end of the line. Clive walks into an area of tenement flats and into nearby countryside. The other man has a house in which Clive's mother also lives. Clive goes into the house and meets his mother, who, unlike her actual appearance, is tall and blond. She wears a priceless diamond choker. (This reminds one of how Clive's faulty ambition chokes him. His empty hopes and daydreams were never based on a solid ground of preparation and experience.)

In the dream it develops that his mother is a widow and that her late husband had been Adolf Eichmann, the Nazi war criminal. Clive transmutes into Eichmann himself and three jet-black brothers wait to attack him. Although Clive has two white body-guards, Clive-alias-Eichmann has his head slashed with a razor. He escapes further attacks and will recover.

Clive can no longer escape his shadow entirely. His alter-ego shows him his mother as a beguiling and bejewelled lady. When a mother who has been unobtainable or unmothering becomes an exciting object, the ego is damaged, needing a more dependable relationship. This may lead in adult life to over-dependency, compulsive sexuality and a need for constant appreciation. Clive fell into this category. The presence of the sadistic Eichmann as both father and son, like an anti-Christ shadow, confirms the darker aspects of Clive's behaviour patterns. The three black brothers are the alter-egos of Clive and his two body-guards. They all seem to be colluding in shadow opposition against their unsupportive and unwell father, except for Clive alone. In reality, Clive sometimes took his father's part at the risk of falling into his father's shadow to do so.

A synchronicity with the I Ching

At session 42, a synchronicity had occurred which caused me to reflect about the case. Clive consulted the *I Ching* and threw Hexagram 42 named the 'I/Increase'. I noticed that he brought in Hexagram 42 to our session number 42. The odds against this numerical synchronicity are great. This alerted me and I calculated changing lines from his throws which moved to Hexagram 58, the 'Joyous/Lake'. Clive's question was to ask the I Ching if he should go abroad permanently or remain in London. This obviously indirectly referred to whether or not to continue the analysis. Therefore I was involved and I took a closer look at the Chinese oracle.

I noticed that the lower trigram of Hexagram 42 concerns the first son which fits Clive, but not me, as I am a second son. The changing lines tried to correct an unfavourable relation to the upper trigram which concerns spirit, or anima, and the way it can help the world. If what was needed in session 42 of the therapy was a change to Hexagram 58, then perhaps my counter-transference was involved with the changing lines. These lines concerned the need for a firmness in the middle way, a resolve over doubts and the danger. I saw the doubt and the danger for my task as being Clive's general narcissistic arrest. The I Ching reported that the danger was strongly enough underpinned. Although that encouraged me concerning my counter-transference at the time, Clive's Hexagram 42 suggested that his unfavourable anima was a problem in his transference to the situation (which included his transference to me). I tried to further incorporate this fact into my counter-transference and I made an effort to defuse this negativity in Clive through a more conscious position in my analytical stance. Not only did the I Ching help me to analyse the transference but it gave me advice for my counter-transference. This was achieved by studying both the Hexagrams and perusing how the situation moved between them and relating that to the transference/counter-transference situation as it moved between us in the therapy.

The archetypal intervention of the sandplay

I have turned to occasional use of the sandplay in this analysis because the absence of the maternal temenos had given Clive's psyche the menace of *an open space*. His ego didn't have a protective temenos around it. Although he was not agoraphobic, his environment always seemed to operate like a threatening void. The sandbox is a free but protected space, with its four sides acting like clear boundaries. As the unconscious archetypal union of the parents had been frustrated by early events in Clive's infancy, I wanted to use the sandplay to help constellate a more holding temenos since Clive's verbalization was 'all over the place' and eminently vague if volatile.

Gerhard Adler writes on the negative mother problem and I quote:

> The actual mother has proved insufficient, and has thus constellated the negative great mother. Then the infant finds it too difficult to identify with mother and suffers from lack of primal containment. In the end the infant has not succeeded in producing a secure enough ego, and the ego is, as it were, left without its proper skin, without its own protective temenos.
>
> (Adler 1979)

The sandplays Clive made during his therapy represented a general image of the situation at the exact point in time when each was made. When he began the analysis, his father and mother archetypes had not been projected in image, through the ego, onto the real parents. Neumann, in his book *The Child* (1973), calls such an ego situation the 'distress-ego'. This distress-ego, which is what Clive brought into analysis, compensates for its weak position by wanting instant gratification and by having a low threshold to the tolerance of frustration. Clive walked out of jobs more than once simply through frustration. That he needed money for alimony payments never bothered him. Meier-Seethaler (1982) has written that when a mother (and in this case a cousin) has rejected a child, they convey to it a 'basic feeling that the world is unlovable ... also the conviction that the child is not deserving of love'. The reinforcement of narcissistic self-consciousness represents a defence against the Terrible Mother. Guilt feelings accompany this and a vicious circle develops which Neumann (1973) describes in this way: '... ego-rigidity, aggression and negativism alternate with feelings of forsakenness, inferiority and unlovedness, each set of feelings intensifying the other'. Forsakenness exacerbates the ego to egocentricity and narcissistic functioning.

The sandplays

I want to describe briefly the four sandplays Clive made. This work indicates the way a Jungian analyst can combine the use of verbal therapy and sandplay material. What is achieved here shows how separate and yet how concurrent and important the sum of both techniques can be to the analytical work. If the dreams centred on the healing of childhood wounding, the sandplays sort out archetypal images in symbolic statements of basic importance to the interpretation of the 'distress-ego' so apparent in this case.

Sandplay 1

We see in the first sandplay made during the third week of analysis a great movement diagonally across the box from the lower left-hand corner to the upper right-hand corner (see Plate 9). From the depths of the archetypal left corner a red stone with the Great Mother's face looking at the bridge is before the three stacked stones. Two wooden ceremonial animals guard the Great Mother; an Indian horse and elephant suggesting great sustaining power in this archetypal image. We have seen the patient's mother relationship to be negative so we can assume that the child being born in the centre needs to be the symbolic child, the historical child and the child needing restoration within the analytic and sandplay process.

Animals and fighters move from the direction of the negative archetypal mother to struggle in order to free consciousness from the grip of the unconscious. There is great libido within the figures in the lower right corner moving up towards the distressed and battle-torn ego area of the upper right corner.

On the left the golden turtle suggests the slow natural evolution of archetypal images that are making a slow march across the space to the ego-centre. The turtle has the rounded top of heaven and the square bottom of the earth; this suggests the lubricity of the female vulva which in alchemy represents the *massa confusa*!

The salamander on the bridge is a lizard inhabiting the element of fire. It gives a paroxism of the indulged imagination that created the picture. Around the distressed ego-area are the stag and the brown horse, both mediators of energies between heaven and earth. The stag represents the cyclic regeneration of life with the cycle of the antlers that come and go.

The monsters show the danger of destruction by women upon

the patient. They are base powers seething in anger with high libido. The ego-corner is one step from chaos and the fascination of evil *per se* within the patient.

The bright orange flame is an eruption of panic in the ego. Behind it is the tree of life, an inexhaustible (generic) force of the life of the cosmos in an upward trend. The tree of life was guarded by monsters at the East Gate of the Babylonian Heaven (i.e., this is the east side of the sandbox). This life-tree was thought to contain the knowledge of both good and evil. As such, the tree can be considered a cross of redemption.

In many ways the first picture is prognostic. It shows the problem of the negative mother and other forces of inner conflict and rage. It suggests that only a new symbolic birth can prevent the fiery distress of forces from impinging upon a distressed and confused ego.

Sandplay 2

The arresting study of the anima condition was made after three months of therapy. At the far left of the upper corner a lion, demure with a purple necklace, rests by the stone like the solar lion guarding the Ark in Egypt (see Plate 10). He marks the death/rebirth place of anima in the patient's psyche. As forces of great libido pour out from the crypt, there is danger if the monsters were to turn around. But they spew forth into the free psychic space.

The hippopotamus represents the mother principle becoming reborn within psyche. The bear and the ape-man suggest perilous aspects of the instincts of the unconscious, which remain cruel, crude and destructive within the anima's dynamic force-field.

Hopefully this incredibly strong catharsis of anima elements will enable the mother hippo to start a more positive anima development within the personality structure of the client. Until now the sado-masochistic tendencies in the patient have tended to overrule less neurotic possibilities and the tendencies represented by the solar lion.

This is a very clear evocation of the male negative anima in image – the clearest picture in my entire archives revealing a mostly negative anima.

Sandplay 3

After six months the patient constructed this sandplay which he entitled 'The land of the archetypes' (see Plate 11).

The patient crosses a bridge to the temenos or central core of a place where he conceptualizes several archetypal images. A carved golden gate marks the entrance. To the upper left, the standing slab of greenstone 'represents my mother and the dark grey hat-stone represents my father'. Behind the dry screen of the honeycomb is a beautiful multi-coloured glass piece; it is the 'source of all I would like to do and be. It is placed on a golden tray', said Clive.

The dried-out honeycomb certainly suggests that the cruel and extremely difficult personal circumstances of the patient need 'a taste of honey' – if ever a patient did, Clive did. The multi-coloured stone may represent the anima in its potential flowering and trans-formation. This had not happened at the time of the sandplay but projective material of this kind often presages developmental possi-bility by many months and indicates the patient's *aspiration* as well.

The man in the sandplay is free to move in any direction he may wish in this reunification of an archetypal ground within the client. This sandplay is a temenos of Self.

Sandplay 4

At ten months a mandala construction is dominated by the urchin shell (see Plate 12). Urchin shells are considered to bring good luck to a journey. They are thought to have a mystic centre which rises upwards like a new generation rising out of the death of the preceding one.

In its interior the urchin shell contains a five-sided starfish. This five-sidedness does not yet point to the spiritual solidarity of quaternity symbols but the five-sided figure is believed to rise up towards the point of origin. I believe that is what religious feeling does dynamically. The starfish is a fertility source and clearly related to the aspects of the moon. These central symbolical ideas fit the patient very well.

To the right of the centre is a working man (the patient), a woman and a lion. The lion is tame and moving on the left side of the patient. These figures are flanked from behind by the dried-out honeycomb and the dark stone hat of the father from the previous sandplay. Red Indians are threatening them from across the water.

Stones and a crystal line the left side of the box.

The lion is reminiscent of the one in the second sandplay. I see him as a masculine energy relating to the integration of the client's negative anima problem. This sandplay suggests that repair and restoration has actually begun of the childhood and later traumas in the patient's psyche.

The ongoing situation

The present state of therapy is in a hiatus. Clive went on holiday after leaving his job and did not return for many months due to family complications and his need to continue searching for a path. He went abroad to a remote religious centre which may be a test of his religious beliefs. On the other hand, away-ness keeps him from being sued for back alimony payments, from his analysis, and from looking for further development. These negative attempts to free the individuality are never better described than by Jung in Volume VII. He mentions how one can turn the superhuman responsibility of the prophet one worships into the unworthiness of the humble disciple. Jung describes mental laziness as a virtuous basking in the sun of a divine master. As to religious centres, the disciples may stick together there, as Jung writes, 'not out of love but for the very understandable purpose of effortlessly confirming their own convictions by engendering the air of collective agreement' (Jung 1961a pp. 170–1).

Before Clive went away he told me he could no longer maintain sexual promiscuity spiritually. This indicates a first break-through towards the possible seeking of real relationship. In his letters, Clive spontaneously acknowledges a shadow problem and a sense of a long individuation ahead. If this is real in him, and only time will test that, it would seem that in spite of the enormous obstacle of a negative infantile narcissism, which was untreated for thirty years, there is a slow and quiet process of ego-strengthening in the therapeutic situation. Clive has expressed gratitude for this. Clive eventually returned from abroad and arranged for regular sessions to resume. At the second session he suddenly announced he was leaving for yet another religious centre abroad. We parted cordially. Orthodox priests had told Clive that Jung was an 'infidel'. He was not well enough to realize that this allegation was untrue.

The ego in psychotherapy that includes the religious instinct as such

Each person must make his own experiments, his own mistakes and successes upon the path of life. There is error in each man's vision of life as no one has found the final truth. In the Western tradition, theology has been dominated either by tenets of belief (dogma and doctrine) or by the 'imitatio Christi' relating more to the pieties of everyday life and to the warmth between 'I and Thou'. In doctrinal theology religion's images come under the control of the mind; in pietist theology, the meanings of religion are felt to be very personal. In both these views the ego's perspectives dominate the matter of interpretation. Persons having ego damage will use an *ego-theology* as a defence mechanism to monopolize the imaginal in religion and pull it away from the psychic individuation of soul.

Both Freud and Jung believed, in their separate ideations, that a science of the soul (in its theological aspect) could only be realized upon one's own self.

> But such a way would be different ... from the approach of various pietisms, since it is not a matter of linking religious content to ego's biography or to personal experience. Rather, it is a likening of the images of religion to the autonomous pathologies of soul over which ego has little will-control and about which ego can make very little sense.
>
> (Miller 1980)

Religious images can be used to further understand the self. Jung's contribution in *Psychology and Religion* (1969b) leaves one in no doubt about this. The heart/mind split can be healed when one senses imaginally, combining both aspects, and religious image can help a healthy ego to achieve transpersonal ideation. There is a strong case to support the idea that religious meaning is not so much located 'in the historical past nor in the eschatological future, but here and now, not in ego, but just where ego is wounded, where its perspectives are deepened soul-wise' (Miller 1980).

The danger in Clive's spiritual search within dogma and possibly within piety is that a damaged ego often settled for a religious compulsive neurosis. Psychic compulsion in Clive's travels may overcome the natural consciousness of inner obligation to a spiritual life. All neurosis points to a loss of reality. When Clive gave up the responsibility to help his young son, he sidestepped a part of reality that should have been suffered through. Instead it was pushed back into the unconscious. Thus a developmental phase is avoided and psychic functions are correspondingly underdeveloped. This situation leads to a disassociation between conscious and unconscious which Clive needed to act out by leaving his analytical work as well as other relationships and which may result in 'psychic fragmentation, contradictory behaviour, even incomprehensible inverse experience and attitudes' (Rudin 1968, p. 161) In Clive's conscious strivings to love God and be united to Him, he may one day be able to offer God what his narcissistic ego damage as yet prevents him offering Man.

The neurosis of prolonged ego damage, where it remains consistent throughout the first half of life, is a product of an underdevelopment of the authentic image of man. It can delay the connection to consciousness of the archetypal God-image lying in the ground of being in the collective unconscious. Thus the groundwork for the second half of life is in jeopardy. 'Among all my patients in the second half of life ... there has not been one whose problem in the last resort was not that of finding a religious outlook on life' (Jung 1933). In Jungian analysis, the area of religious image and its development approaches the task of spiritual guidance whether analysts care to carry such a burden or not. It would behove the religious practitioner to be aware of and use the unique relationship of psychotherapy and religion as much as it would behove contemporary Jungian analysts to reawake to the fullness of their task – a task that can bond the religious outlook to a ground of *psychological becoming* both in themselves and in their patients.

In this analytical case I have tried to indicate one way of working: my main emphasis was on symbolic transformation and integration of dream material with child development seen as the unfolding of the archetypes which, in this case, was severely impeded by the analysand's ego position. My client was, however, able to achieve a partial resolution of infantile fixations and complexes within an analysis which focused on the deepest and most genuine experience of the symbolic contents of dreams and of the archetypal images released in the sandplays.

3. THE STORY OF MARIE: A MATURE WOMAN IN GRIEF WORKS THROUGH HER MOURNING PROCESS

This is a case involving a mature woman who came to sandplay for a specific reason: to work through grief, separation and mourning. A French woman of fifty years whom I shall name 'Marie' commuted to London to do a series of sandplays. It was after the death of her older sister 'Edith' that Marie wished to express her deep grief and mourning within sandplay therapy. Edith had died six months earlier from cancer after a long illness.

The two sisters were born of aristocratic parents and grew up outside Versailles in an upper-bourgeois household and spent their young summers with their parents and friends on an ancestral wine-growing estate in the Ardèche. There Marie who had studied painting from an early age spent her days painting the southern French landscape. Edith was very extroverted and fun-loving although an excellent student, while Marie was artistic, serious and thoughtful. Their quietly upper-class life protected their inseparable relationship which continued even after both married. Edith married an heir to a large country estate in lower Normandy and her husband played the French stock exchange and managed the estate. Marie married a quiet medical student who rose up to become a leading eye surgeon in Paris connected to several hospitals. They lived in the ancestral house in Versailles while Edith and her husband lived in a triplex in the Quai d'Orsay in Paris. Each was the mother of two children and both retained their childhood characters and special closeness with one another over the years. When Edith died, Marie was overwhelmed by grief.

When Marie arrived I met a well-dressed, calm and sad woman. Her Chanel suit was black. We spoke at length of the last months of her sister's suffering and of her last agony at her sister's death. Her husband and children had been sensitive to Marie's grief but she wanted to express her feelings in a therapeutic setting outside her own superb painting which had grown over the years to a professional level and therefore was not the psychological medium she needed to use in therapy. She began her sandplays at weekly intervals.

Sandplay 1

In this balanced and rich landscape we get a diagnostic preview of a positive prognostic result to the sandplay process (see Plate 13). Six ponds announce a deep link in the patient to the unconscious symbolized by water and the invisible underwater currents.

The relationship of sister to sister is everywhere echoed in dyadic pairs: two storks, two swans, two gods at the centre top and two Chinese women in the upper centre.

'I am the lavender Chinese woman in the centre,' said Marie. A devout Roman Catholic, Marie expressed her religious and philosophic awareness by placing three Oriental goddesses across the landscape: one is playing the mandolin, one is spinning and one is, like Kuang Lin, in repose. These feminine aspects of a meditative character will come again many times.

Several male gods as ancient scribes and wise men line both the right and left edges of the sandplay. Two male gods overlook the scene from the top. Marie's energies are spiritualized in her grief as evidenced by the white horse and the golden horse. The many birds are messengers between heaven and earth and the ten wise men are witnesses to the coming ritual expression of grief.

In the lower left an Indian chief with a full panoply of white feathers next to a golden horse suggests enough *animus* strength in the patient to undertake the sandplay process to a positive conclusion. Animus is the psychic image in woman from her unconscious archetypal structure which underlies woman's 'masculine' aspects. The animus has great value as linking to Marie's creative potential and her individuation through the mourning process. Jung believed the animus to be closely associated to the archetype of meaning so that its projected images contain a strong psychic reality for the individual.

Marie's use of the Indian chieftain suggests that her ego is leading and deciding, like a chieftain, what is best expressed in the sandplay and that the series will be based on experience. I say this because traditionally the initiatory experiences of the Indian chieftains were believed to be difficult and required both achievement and wisdom.

Near the turquoise Chinese lions, a symbol of high defence and guardedness, is an open space or burial ground. This is the temenos of the separation and death experience. It represents both this fact of the sister's death and the sandplay space in which the deepest healing needs to take place. On the lower left, a Chinese man is followed by a spirited Chinese woman dancing. It is prognostically important that a stag is nearby, a symbol for a messenger of the gods often representing the pure soul searching for re-baptism, the Grail, or the Way of Ascent. Rejuvenation is indicated by the stag's annually-new antlers. In Britain and sometimes in France antlers are placed on graves to indicate that the deceased will have eternal life. A kangaroo with a baby in its pouch reaffirms the need in the patient for a rebirth experience arising like a Phoenix out of the ashes of her grief-stricken psyche.

Sandplay 2

A Chinese woman who is the patient stands next to her husband near the golden horse and a golden lamb (see Plate 14). 'I want to lie down with the lamb,' said Marie. The lamb symbolizes gentleness, meekness and purity. The theme of mystic rebirth surrounds the unblemished innocence of the lamb. Christ is suffering the passion and in the triumph of resurrection is 'living within' the golden lamb. There is also an important Chinese meaning here for the lamb indicates *filial* piety in the Far East. Both Edith and Marie had strong family piety in their love for one another and in their love of family.

Here the Holy Family – Joseph, Mary and the Christ Child – serve as a spiritual basis for grappling with the pyramid tombstone of her sister. This is the eternal burial place, fit for a Pharaoh, and the white and gold animals nearby symbolize the spiritualized energies surrounding the atmosphere.

On the left side is a well indicating the importance of human bodily nourishment during the mourning process, and the camels approach it eagerly. They have survived the desert (or an experience of separation from life source or water) and they come also as the traditional mascots of my sandplay room because of their knowledge of the sand!

Sandplay 3

In the upper left-hand corner a golden screen and to its right, a golden obelisk form the background for seven male gods and in front of them, Marie's primal family: her mother, sister, and father (see Plate 15). To the lower left the three Chinese goddesses symbolizing the number three as the solution of a conflict posed by dualism, life or death.

This echoes the upturned triangle around the Christ Child, here on a crystal, archetypal plinth as the Eternal Child. Joseph and Mary have a family totem between them suggesting the primal family of Marie is now three in number, not four. Three represents the growth of unity within but a problem still remains. The lion, or energic process, is leaving the tomb and walking away (upper right). Had the lion stayed with the Lamb (Christ Child) a paradoxical state would be indicated. But Marie is feeling a powerful problematic. The solar energy of the lion as masculine, hence her own animus, is leaving her psychic energy system. She is depressed and witnessing the end of the golden time when her family was whole and complete.

The Indian chieftain is present again with a swan behind him. A swan is solar and announces the dawn of day; its whiteness is sincerity, breadth, spirit, and it represents the Virgin Mary. Some of the animus strength remains present in the swan and in the Indian chieftain. The supreme swan, the *paramahamra* is the Self. As the female principle (it is hermaphroditic in essence) the swan is sacred to the goddess of death.

Sandplay 4

The 'Grim Reaper' dominates the sandplay (see Plate 16). With a thrust of his arm holding the sword, mere mortals are cut down in death. Marie said, 'On the seven plinth stones is the story of what I must do'. Here the patient has a break-through to self-knowledge and senses the task ahead in the therapy. Taking the objects on the plinths from left to right, first is the golden horse sitting on a blue egg. The cosmic egg of spiritual rebirth needs the energies of the golden horse to be born. Next is a red flowering cherry-tree and on the third plinth a white flowering apple-tree. Growth and flowering within the mourning process will be needed to contend with Edith's death. Next is the serene Quang Lin statue, essence of a complete and serene femininity. On the fifth plinth a sage owl with red eyes sits. The owl represents death and wisdom as a night-bird gazing into the darkness of loneliness and despair.

Next comes the peacock, its glorious tail feathers symbolizing the development and further flowering of the personality with distinctiveness and, as well, the immortality of a soul in Paradise. Moving backwards to the right we have a stone with multi-coloured glass on top. I have found over the years that women patients most often use this as a flowering of the animus, its base or archetypal stone being topped with refracting coloured glass. A white cow and the goddess playing the mandolin are the feminine witnesses to a return of animus strength as Marie faced the Grim Reaper with her own stages of developmental individuation.

The empty shells suggest a path of austere loneliness still to be borne but three blue horses offer energies of thinking and spiritual energy that lead up to the peacock with its green feathers of sensation function and its blue feathers resonating with thinking, healing and the sky of heaven as well as the deep blue sea.

Sandplay 5

In the upper left-hand corner is a white Oriental fisherman representing the age of Pisces, or of Christ in the West, and an echo of the Grim Reaper of the last sandplay (see Plate 17). The golden coffin of Edith is at his feet. A golden screen backs a silver tree of life in the upper centre, in front of which two immortal glass love birds sit on a crystal representing eternal love which lives beyond the grave.

Marie said, 'In front are seven problems again represented as animals. I don't know what they mean'. Starting with the white elephant in the centre, this is the animal that appeared to Queen Maya to announce the birth of the Buddha. Compassion, love and kindness are indicated by the elephant, who is central to the other animals. The white elephant is solar, hence masculine, and here shows Marie's animus to be intact and a part of the procession of energies represented.

Starting with the left three animals, from lower to upper, the squirrel is a bringer of rain, water and snow. The nourishment of the feminine through her sister is here denoted by Marie as now bereft and in need of replenishment from other sources. Squirrels mean fertility in Japan, the very quality that grief makes one forget and become unaware of fertility's existence. The empty, freezing flatness of grief needs an augury of watering.

Next upwards is the frog with green eyes. The frog is both lunar and a rain-bringer. Marie needs these two qualities restored to her psyche. As a frog rises from the water to the land it is a renewal of life. Marie needs psychic resurrection. This frog's green eyes symbolize the reproductive power of nature and may comment on Marie's longevity compared to her sister.

Above the frog is the rabbit, another lunar animal suggesting Marie's deep wound from the loss of feminine contact with Edith. The rabbit can live on the moon mythically and also with the Earth Mother. However, the rabbit is the trickster of the American Indians, so it can trick Marie's animus as she has twice used the Indian chieftain for her unconscious masculine spirit in earlier sandplays. As all the animals are directed towards the right side of the box we can hope these forces are becoming more conscious to Marie.

To the right of the elephant, from lower to higher, comes a black and white cow with a full udder. The cow suggests the Great Mother in her positive and negative characteristics. She is the maternal instinct nourishing all the moon goddesses in her lunar aspect. The cow is both celestial (moon) and chthonic (earth). Marie is the mother of two. Her maternal instincts reappear but she too needs the milk and rain of the Great Mother cow. In Egypt, Isis had a gilt-image of a cow at the mourning rites for Osiris.

Above the cow is the blue horse. This is Marie's body with the spirit as *she who would ride her*. The horse pulls the sun chariot by day and is linked to Helios. In its magical element, the horse figured in rain-making ceremonies and in chthonic cults associated with burial rites. There is a sense of readiness for action quite new to Marie in the mourning period, but remaining unconscious as to what action to take, hence the sitting horse. The horse is also the tree of death, relating to the silver tree of life in the top centre of the sandplay. The modern Persian word for coffin means 'wooden horse'. The blue colour relates to the sea-blue as the unconscious and to qualities of rich, healing blue.

The last animal is the resting lioness. Here the Magna-Mater, the Black Virgin, the All-Mother, Rhea, or Astarte symbolize protection and quiet nobility. Marie is protected by a noble family heritage and this is supportive to her belief in a future after the fierce suffering of present grief. The lioness is her libido and is identical metaphorically with the flow of her total psychic energy.

Six Western animals contrast sharply with the sacred white elephant from whose ear the Buddha was born. We see in this sandplay the beginning of movement in those psychic forces which will be healing to the stasis of despair and loss which Marie has borne.

Sandplay 6

Now the patient begins to work through her problem using many figures from past sandplays (see Plate 18). There is a sense of other-worldliness about this sandplay as all the figures are statues or angels except for five Chinese dolls that represent Marie's relatives gathered at Edith's grave in the lower left-hand corner. The love birds command the bottom centre of the picture with three Chinese wise men standing behind like a guard of honour. The centre of the sandplay is dominated by a dark spire. 'This is the spire of death in the land of death,' said Marie.

Three pairs of birds surround the base of the spire as messengers between earth and the land of death. Gathered behind these is an unusual semi-circle of male figures. Joseph is the only recognizable one. The Virgin Mary has so honoured this male group as to stand behind them, indicating as Queen of Heaven a deference to their special task in the land of death.

Who are these figures?

There is an important link here to the *richesse* of Egyptian belief about external parts or figures that meet a man or woman in death. These figures I believe to be projected by Marie's psyche as a part of her psychic economy in dealing with other-worldly aspects of imagining her dead sister's passage. I believe these male figures are the Sahu, the Ka, the Ba, the Khaibit, the Khu and the Sekhem.

We know that the Egyptians believed in a future life. In all periods of research into the ancient pyramid texts, external existence is postulated. Immortality is the oldest Egyptian belief. To renew life in the Other World and exist for millions of years was the wish of everyone. The preservation of the corruptible body in the tomb was connected to life in the world to come. This physical body was called *khat*. This body neither leaves the tomb nor reappears on earth.

In the sandplay, the relatives and seven angels beside Edith's tomb, through the force of their prayers change the physical body to a spiritual body called *sahu*. The sahu body can converse with the soul. It can ascend into heaven and converse with the Gods. In close connection to the physical and spiritual bodies was an abstract personality with an independent existence which could unite or separate from the bodies at will; it was named the *Ka*. It was the movement and power which guided the fortunes of an individual in the hereafter. The tombs always had special chambers where the Ka was honoured. The Ka could eat food and drink.

The *Ba* on the other hand was the 'heart-soul' of the deceased, a refined and ethereal eternal being taking up any shape in heaven or earth it pleased. It could revisit the body in the grave or dwell among perfected souls in heaven.

The *Khaibit* was the shadow of the dead person. It usually was thought to be the shade of the Ba and to accompany it on its journeys. Prayers were offered by mourners that the Khaibit should never be fettered but always free to roam near to the soul.

The *Khu* was another eternal aspect of the dead person's being in Eternity. It is a translucent spirit-soul, more shining and glorious than the Ba. The Khus of the gods lived in heaven and a person's Khu could join them immediately after death.

The *Sekhem* is vital power and exists among the Khus in heaven. It is associated with purity. Sir E.H. Wallis Budge (1960), late keeper of the Egyptian and Assyrian Antiquities in the British Museum, points out that there are no English expressions to convey adequately what Sekhem means in its Egyptian conception except that the god Re was called the 'Great Sekhem', suggesting the powerful element within its meaning.

Marie's six men may indicate these six parts of Edith's immortal nature. Put together they would resemble Edith's animus quite exactly in Egyptian belief.

The fact that the Virgin stands behind and aside from the male figures suggests these representations are healing for Marie. The Virgin is the greatest healer of these 2,000 years together with the Christ Himself, who is obliquely referred to in the pure white fisherman, the man of Pisces or the Christian era. It is by no means rare that a practising Christian will revive from the collective unconscious the sophisticated pagan beliefs of the Egyptian Arabs, a culture of supreme insight and deep religious fervour.

The 'three Graces' look on from the top suggesting a multi-cultural Oriental trinity as an overview to the memorable sandplay. The sacred white elephant presaging Buddha's birth moves majestically towards the centre. Here, then, is a sandplay of Spirit and Hereafter.

Sandplay 7

In the foreground nine angels fall down and are laid out on a barge-like ferry (see Plate 19). Are they dead? Can angels die? Marie just doesn't know. Above them are three precious blue stones: the centre one rests by itself as the Philosopher's Stone, the stone beyond price of individuation within development. To the right the Virgin stands on the stone, witnessing the passage of the 'fallen' angels. To the left is the Chinese goddess with her mandolin. Just above and behind these feminine personages lies Joseph, seemingly asleep and resting from his 'participation mystique' in so many of Marie's sandplays! Behind him is a brown plinth marking his place and then a high statue, at the top centre, of a Buddha head from Java. Now Buddha is given a human face in a shrine backed by the golden screen and two impressive Oriental blue columns. At the upper right-hand corner a white horse rests beneath a small spire, an echo of the spire of death in the last sandplay and the spiritual energies that scene required from Marie's psyche. Sleep, tiredness, and a resting spirit pervade this desert-like atmosphere. Around the sleeping Joseph there are five green marbles, a colour of natural harmony, hope and of a returning sensation towards life to come.

Sandplay 8

Here the Egyptian boat holding Edith's body in heaven travels towards an egg-timer as a gravestone with one of the male spirit figures from Sandplay 6 standing over it (see Plate 20). In the upper right-hand corner Marie's ego is represented as a Chinese lion statue, frozen into a stasis of movement as she contemplates her sister's passage to the land of the unconscious where Marie hopes Edith can be conscious. This boat was built by Marie in France to bring to London to show this memorable and evocative passage. The sands of time in the egg-timer used as a gravestone suggest sand as the arbiter of the bereavement and separation experience that Marie is now beginning to contain.

Sandplay 9

Marie said that the great high purple gate was 'the Gate of the Beyond to the Divine Mother's court' (see Plate 21). She brings a varied landscape of rivers and lakes surrounded by many figures she consciously has used in earlier sandplays. There is an atmosphere of joy in the reappearance of many birds lining the sacred path to the Gate of the Beyond. In the lower right, two Chinese women personify Edith and Marie's bond. Joseph and the Indian chieftain with his tepee flanked by giraffes bring the masculine as witness. Two Chinese goddesses in the lower left bring the feminine as witness.

Beyond the gate where Edith must go is the Divine Mother with one of the male statues just before her. She is flanked by two peacocks showing her royal status.

In Indian mythology the Divine Mother (*Mahasakti*) has three modes of being: (1) as the supreme sakti who links the supreme creation to still unmanifested mystery; (2) as She who creates all beings and directs all of the millions of processes and forces; (3) as the living presence who makes this alive and interposes between human personality and divine nature.

So for Marie's part she is projecting a vision of judgement for Edith from a Divine Mother and represents her in the Indian form rather than as the Virgin Mary, Queen of Heaven.

Often sandplay patients will use Oriental figures to orient their own psychological processes within the sandplay. The Divine Mother of India is thought to be fully incarnate in every human mother and in the kundalini at the base of every human being's vertebral column.

Marie may well herself need the grace of the Divine Mother and wish herself to go through the Gate of the Beyond. In the vivid energy and balance so evident in this sandplay, one senses Marie's depression is lifting and her mourning beginning to give creative force to her sandplay expression.

Sandplay 10

In a sandplay of great power and beauty, Marie places the great solar disc overseeing the grave of Edith (see Plate 22). Edith is seen as alabaster surrounded by white lights. Joseph and six male gods look on as the exotic funeral procession leaves the graveside moving across to the right side. Two Chinese goddesses stand near the grave as Joseph prays. The sacred white elephant is near the five blue horses and a five-level pagoda demarks the area above. The symbolism of five represents man who forms a pentagon with outstretched arms and legs. The pentacle means the whole. It is the Godhead as the central creator of the four great forces. The *hieros gamos* is the marriage of two (feminine) and three (masculine). Five also symbolizes those forces coming alive in Marie as she is able to begin to leave the burial site: meditative expression, religious feeling, and versatility in the sandplays, the quintessence of which she has expressed here.

The upper left-hand corner has the golden screen once more, the Chinese lion and the pyramid with the green stone inside. The stone sharpens its essence as does anything else enclosed within a pyramid.

Sandplay 11

Here is an apotheosis. Marie resurrects Edith and meets her in the centre of the grave which is now elaborated further as a final statement of transcendent reincarnation (see Plate 23). The use of trees, lights, gods and goddesses gives the grave a mystical quality of numinosity. The two peacocks look on from the realm of the Divine Mother (Sandplay 9) and the five blue horses frolic near the silver tree of life.

Seven angels flank the area where from above the two sisters are seen again walking away from an Oriental village. In the lower right-hand corner a rickshaw and a green dancing lady with a golden turtle move slowly off the stage of Marie's imagination. This is farewell and reunion, death as continued life and a final statement of release and recollection on Marie's part.

Marie's work might be summed up in the words of Meister Eckhart: 'the soul is capable of knowing all things in her highest power', namely 'as a clear mirror one sees all things in one image', and so 'not until she knows all there is to be known does she cross over to the Unknown Good' (Evans 1924, p. 419).

This patient, a mature and balanced woman of fifty, achieved her goal of release, recollection and renewal as sandplay added peace of mind to her grief and mourning. Without words and away from all family influence, she found the meditative space in the sandbox to express and discover her pent-up feelings and philosophy. A Roman Catholic, Marie found Oriental imagery which centred her aesthetic and emotional use of the materials, a new experience. Marie expressed deep gratitude for the sandplay therapy and returned to Paris with renewed ego-strength to go on living through her mourning. She had succeeded in expressing essence in terms of her psychological existence and she affirmed in her constructions a sense of the Platonic mortal and immortal status.

Coomaraswamy reminds us, 'Our whole tradition everywhere affirms that there are two in us'; the Hebrew *nefesh* and *ruah* and the Islamic *nafa* and *ruh*, Philo's 'soul', Egyptian Pharaoh and his *Ka*, Chinese outer and inner Sage, Psyche and Pneuma, and Vedantic *atman* and 'self's Immortal Self'. The ultimate question according to Coomaraswamy is 'In whom, when I go hence, shall I be going forth? In my self, or its Immortal Self?' (Coomaraswamy 1977, p. 428).

In the words of Jalalu'd-Din Rumi is one answer; 'Die before you die'. All scriptures insist on freedom from self as spiritually essential at the last.

Marie's mourning for Edith was Marie's dying before she dies, and the sandplay gives a three-dimensional record of that pilgrimage through darkness and heartbreak.

4. THE STORY OF AGNES: A YOUNG GIRL ENTERS PUBERTY AS HER PARENTS DIVORCE

Since we are all in a state of continual change, we normally mark adolescence as a period of more rapid transition between a state of *being* a child and the state of gradually *becoming* an adult. Adolescents find themselves in a marginal position between the former status of the child and the future status of the adult: they are neither. They are seen as so rapidly changing that their status is vague, ambiguous and sometimes disorientated from the viewpoint of general society.

A girl of fourteen was referred to me just as she awaited the inception of her menstruation. Her transitional anxiety was greatly increased as her parents had announced they were divorcing just at that time. Although each of the girl's parents was in analysis, with different Jungian analysts, they inevitably burdened my patient and her younger sister of nine with a series of incidents related to their separation, which added to their daughters' anxieties concerning change in the family unit.

The older daughter asked if she could see a therapist and the mother's analyst made a referral to me for sandplay therapy early one summer. Not only was my young patient, whom I shall call 'Agnes', made anxious by the adolescent crisis of development with its concomitant challenge of menstruation, but the status she had enjoyed within her primal family was now in severe flux. Her father had a mistress and soon the two daughters were to take a holiday with this couple, leaving their real and very depressed mother behind.

Agnes fought these challenges with a high degree of striving. At home she cooked the evening meal each day after a long day at school because her mother was often unable to function and remained in her bedroom in a depressed state for days at a time. At school, Agnes managed her work but was not yet moving socially in the more extroverted group she longed to join. She acted in a young drama group every weekend and there seemed to find new friends and a more independent behaviour, more outgoing than her usual introverted self-consciousness. Her special interests were the French and Italian language courses at school and her dream was to gain her independence one day by becoming a simultaneous translator. Her father was employed by government and she identified with his busy activity and earning power, his independence and his professional sense. She also contained and comprehended a part of her mother's suffering, to quite a remarkable degree: this concerned me because her mother had been raped during the German army's occupation of her continental country of origin and was working through a difficult regressive and withdrawn period in her own analysis. It was this that alerted her analyst to contact me about a possible danger to Agnes of introjection of her mother's persecutory anxieties, just when the threshold of adolescence gave Agnes an initiatory challange and a potential sexual development operating in its own time as her rightful development.

Our working mode together was as follows: initially Agnes brought her dream book and we looked at the dream material, using at first associations from Agnes which tended to remain focused upon her feelings of jealousy of other adolescent girls. They were either more popular at school, or had stable homes, or both. Agnes got up each morning at six o'clock to deliver newspapers to earn holiday money and she told me her impressions of the pleasant, middle-class district where she lived outside of central London. She had been given jurisdiction over her younger sister on weekday evenings, since her mother was heavily medicated and her father often away, and this gave Agnes a truly heavy load of real responsibility.

She presented herself to me, in the first session, with considerable control and self-possession in what she described about her life and asked both for sandplay and for talks about her dream material. Her stability was an ongoing reality; because so much was unintentionally denied her at home in this crisis situation, I did not deny her the mode of working in the sessions she asked for which, theoretically, seemed to me too heavy-going for her at first. I am restricting my description of the case to her sandplays because I carefully phased out some of the verbal therapy gradually over the summer and used a delayed-interpretation in sandplay (see Weinrib 1983). In the beginning she needed dream work as well and I contained that using the holding and mirroring aspect of my working personality principally.

Here is her first sandplay description, made in the first session, which her father attended for the first ten ,minutes of joint discussion, after which he waited for Agnes in my waiting room. He did not attend the sessions again but brought Agnes by car (a one-hour journey) once a week to my consulting rooms in central London.

Sandplay 1

Agnes said that the green Chinese dancing lady crossing the lower bridge in the upper left-hand corner was herself (see Plate 24). She was approaching her mother who needed a rickshaw to carry her 'as she is extremely tired and depressed'. The Oriental buildings behind Agnes are 'a village in which my house is the smallest one along to the right'. Agnes said the walrus with tusks to the right at the top 'is my friend'. He can come up out of the water and 'visit me at my house'. This indicates that an energy that can live in the water (or the unconscious) can be used more consciously and can move up onto the sandy beach and beyond.

On the fishing boat Agnes said the fisherman was her father. The home situation is indicated here. The father was supporting his family but a date had been set when he would move out and live with his mistress whom he intended to marry. This woman had been the best friend of his wife so Agnes was presented with the anxiety of continuing on in the family home with her mother and younger sister without her father's daily presence. Thus an archetypal situation of primal family unity and security was to be broken and basic change was imminent.

It is interesting that a large crystal is placed in an orchard of trees in the lower left-hand corner. Jung believed that in man's collective unconscious there are primordial collective forms that influence the way conscious material is experienced. Jung compared this to a crystal, which Agnes has used to indicate the depth of her archetypal image projection of impending primal family change.

The form of these archetypes is perhaps comparable to the axial system of a crystal which predetermines ... the crystalline formation in the saturated solution, without itself possessing a material existence. This existence first manifests itself in the way that ions and then the molecules arrange themselves ... the axial system determines ... merely the stereometric structures, not ... the concrete form of the individual crystal ... and just so the archetype possesses ... an invariable core of meaning that determines its manner of appearing always only in principle, never concretely.

(Jung 1939, p. 79)

On the upper right above the boat we see an octopus. The octopus often heralds the spiral, a sense of ascent and descent in a patient's psyche as one begins sandplay for the first time. Related to the mystic centre, the octopus indicates Agnes' potential fertility. She is waiting for and expecting her first menstrual period soon, but as yet she is pre-pubertal with an intensely virginal quality of 'waiting'. Nature's fertility rituals are usually 'veiled' and a death sacrifice required. In Agnes' family, her mother is bedridden by severe black depression. Wailing and weeping as at a fertility rite are sounds Agnes knows well.

In the sandplay she greets her ailing mother on a bridge. This transitional bridge suggests a passage during the coming sandplay process that will bring Agnes both closer to her mother in her suffering but also closer to womanhood through the expected start of menstruation.

Underneath the friendly walrus are several cockle shells, feminine symbols of Aphrodite and other sea-goddesses. It is said that poetic imagination can 'sail' in cockle-shell boats. Here we have an indication of Agnes' expressive use of sandplay to come in a first sandplay containing a dynamic presaging of the new and more mature relationship she must reach with her mother and father placed so far apart on the left and right sides of the sandplay. This first sandplay hints at the feminine pilgrimage Agnes will discover in the sandplay process. She will need to don a cockle-shell hat, metaphorically, as did the Galician pilgrims walking to Compostela in Spain to honour St James. It seemed to me her 'patron saint' would have to be the sandplay therapy itself if not her therapist, too!

Sandplay 2

Here Agnes descends to a preverbal level and indicates how the family energies (as five blue horses) are now constellated (see Plate 25). The horses are each a family member plus the father's mistress. This woman is cautiously accepted or liked by Agnes, but more in a spirit of riding out the family storm with fondness towards all than with total conviction at this stage.

Of the three archaic stone circles, the one to the right shows the problem uppermost at subliminal level of projection for Agnes – her mother's loss of her marriage. One blue horse stands on a grave facing a plinth stone to timeless serenity marking the death of the mother's married relationship to the father. This blue horse (as the mother's energy) just manages to stand in desolation at the loss of the husband's love and commitment to the original family life and home.

In the upper centre Agnes felt that possibly she and her sister were dealing also with some depression indicated by the two dark grey half-buried stones. The blue horse with its front legs on one of the dark stones is a representation of Agnes' energy and overview of her younger sister's energy. Agnes was in full charge of cooking evening meals after a long day at school and she commandeered her sister's help when possible. She prepared meals on a tray for her bedridden mother at this time and was showing a fine discipline, flexibility and energy to cope with these extra and responsible daily tasks.

In the lower left-hand corner in a varied circle of stones are two blue horses which Agnes thought might represent her father and his new sexual partner. The horses go around on the stones in a circle. There is an archaic archetypal configuration and feel to these three primordial groupings; the grieving abandoned wife in middle age, the bond of kinship between two young sisters and the eternal coniunctio of male and female as the primal base of human pro-creation, past or present, prefiguring Agnes' entry to puberty.

Agnes had dived deeply into her personal awareness of the situation but her use of the stones and the atmosphere of profound symbolism suggests that the collective unconscious is projected as well as the personal unconscious in this powerful but desolate sandplay. A sense of dying to be reborn through depressive experience is suggested.

Agnes had to choose between a holiday with her father and his friend near the tors on Dartmoor or to stay with her ill mother. The beginning of splitting in her emotional life was upon her.

Sandplay 3

This sandplay has the frozen quality of virginal waiting for the first pain of menstruation not yet arrived for Agnes (see Plate 26). The Oriental image suggests that Agnes is orientating to her coming adulthood in a kind of incubation.

Agnes said that she is the central upper green lady walking towards the village. Her mother is represented both on the horizon behind her in a rickshaw and ahead of her resting under a sun umbrella in a red dress. Agnes is here a water-carrier, a bringer of the sustenance of the new feminine attitudes of her adolescent generation. She deeply respected and comprehended her mother's suffering at this time. She also knew that her ongoing relationship with her father depended on her accepting his friend as a kind of 'other' relative. She went on holiday with her father as an act of security-seeking with some misgivings.

On the frozen lake dominated by a Chinese lion statue, indicating a guarded spiritual island in the middle of the reflective water, two fishing-boats quietly float side by side. Agnes said this was herself and her sister waiting for an uncertain outcome. High up in the upper left-hand corner a silver tree suggests spiritual growth in the temenos-like village area in front where Agnes as carrier of the new feminine spirit must enter soon as a menstruating fertile being.

In 'The Landscape of Virginity' Robert Sardello (1982) has written, quoting John Layard, that 'virginity refers to the transformation of a basic instinct for union with the mother into a desire for spiritual union with the soul; virginity is a primary telos of the individual soul'. Within virginal consciousness there is a sense of spiritual purity here represented by the placid beauty of this sandplay. Its frozen quality may impede psychological development until the instincts break through to new energies of the life force. This sandplay is a stasis where movement barely exists. Menstruation seems pending now like the calm before a storm.

Sandplay 4

Events were moving rapidly. Agnes was depressed as her father had moved to London with his new partner and spent only two nights a week at home. Soon he would move out altogether. Each week on her way to my consulting rooms in central London, Agnes would ride by a high hill which she associated only with the journey to therapy. She pictures it in this sandplay as a symbol of her positive transference to sandplay therapy and to me (see Plate 27). She put four white horses on it as the last image or vestige of the primal family. With her father's departure soon there would be three women at home and no man.

On the upper right is a bridge to this analytical work and below and downwards, two young white swans indicate, according to Agnes, 'my sister and myself in the river of life'. The family-to-be at home is represented on the lower left by three white birds: the two swans again as the sisters, and their mother as an affectionate duck on land, too tired to swim.

On the upper left a yellow car enters the urban London area symbolizing Agnes' intuitive ego as she rides to her sandplay session. On the upper right the bridge near the yellow-roofed house has sand deliberately sprinkled on it to indicate that the sandplay, too, is a journey within.

The white animals also suggest the virginal quality just before a young woman is initiated to the blood of menstruation. The mountain on which the spiritual white horses rest is swollen and almost pregnant with the sensation of the menses to come.

Agnes has begun her real journey into a budding maturity. The entire sandplay has a mandala image of the circular hill within the sandbox. A green car passes behind the horses, the symbolic colour of the sensation function.

Sandplay 5

At this session Agnes came in with a new self-made dress of sophisticated style. Her hair-style was also more carefully wrought. Her father had spoken to me telling me she had reached her first menstrual period. Her own relief that her cycle had started seemed to irradiate her being. The woman in the child had rapidly appeared. Tellingly enough, three young men had shown interest in her at school in a more personal way than she had before attracted and there was a sense of excitement in her new enthusiasm and energy for school-life.

In the upper right-hand corner, Agnes represented these three boyfriends as three stags overlooking a North American Indian family (father, mother and papoose) before their tepee (see Plate 28). Two white horses graze nearby near the water's edge in which a walrus and hippopotamus stand near the shore. On the small island near the lower left-hand corner, a crocodile is hidden among the trees.

Let us start by interpreting the animal energies. The crocodile reflects Agnes' new fecundity. It rests on an island, not yet requiring to move to any action. The hippopotamus represents health and vigour in a possible heir (as in Egyptian hieroglyphics) and echoes motherhood as a new possibility; Trueret was the goddess of maternity in Egypt and is sometimes indicated as a hippo, the mother of Osiris. The hippopotamus can also suggest repressed anger in Agnes towards her father who has now left the household forever. Hippos kill their own fathers to 'copulate' with their mothers. In this case, Agnes' animus, or spiritually masculine principle in archetypal image (also represented by the stags) is lurking by her friendly walrus from her first sandplay.

The two horses suggest sexual instincts as man plus horse equals man plus his animal instincts. Horseflesh was sacramentally eaten by the king (or one's ego) after his symbolic rebirth from the Mare-headed mountain goddess (suggested in Sandplay 4 as well). Horses also represent the cyclic phenomena of nature, hence menstruation. The general characteristics of all horses reflect Agnes' new potential: as fertility, as mother symbol, as love and lasciviousness, fidelity and sensitivity. A strong and useful animal, the horse can also indicate Agnes' strength and extra tasks in adapting to her mother's household.

In the new baby of the Indian couple, we see the potential of Agnes' child-bearing capacity now become reality. The stark simplicity of this primal level of energy representation shows Agnes' increased grounding into her instinctual base as primal, fecund young woman.

Sandplay 6

Here the brown horse on the bridge at the top represents Agnes' new ego energies, blossoming into dyadic pairs across the landscape of the sandplay (see Plate 29). A very feminine quality pervades the composition. At the middle of the left-hand side-edge of the sandbox, a golden urn – the container of the feminine spirit – is guarded by a white Chinese god and goddess. Two birds, two fish and two flying ducks bring the theme of duplication forward; like a reflection in a mirror, it echoes reality, a symbol of consciousness.

Agnes is growing fast in her awareness of herself. She has suddenly become popular at school, voted into a class honour by her classmates and she spreads throughout this sandplay positive symbols of personality: the owl of wisdom, a woman's golden mirror (her new feminine narcissism and use of cosmetics and perfume), varied small shells of hidden feminine qualities still emerging, a ripe tomato plant, a jewelled box (the vagina as potential receptacle), and other elements of value to the feminine. A circle of mauve-coloured stones in the lower right corner indicate a nucleus or the egg of cyclic ovum. Circles of stones were thought by primitive peoples to be a fertility manifestation of the divine.

A coiled snake rests before the silver tree on the right-hand side of the sandbox – the resting potential sexuality at the foot of a tree of life. In the top right-hand corner is a touchstone which is symbolic of increased ego-awareness of the body. It is 'fixed' in the consciousness, and opposed to wandering thoughts, spirits and desires. Agnes' new concentration at school is bringing her much higher marks than earlier. Her confidence is increased as she approaches her fifteenth birthday. There is a sense in this sandplay of the reintegration of personality elements that is initiated at this time. She is discovering her potential and a new successful image at school.

Sandplay 7

Created directly after Agnes' fifteenth birthday party, this sandplay represents the problematics of her late adolescence to the same extent that the previous sandplay represented the more fulfilled aspects.

Now grotesque and lesser known living figures challenge the psyche (see Plate 30). At the top centre two clowns and two 'goons', purple and orange, look on 'foolishly'. To the upper right, shell figures dance a joyous dance while two spacemen join in. These men represent the male mystery to Agnes. In asbestos suits, their bodies remain indistinct. Agnes as yet has no carnal knowledge of men's genitalia. Beneath the spacemen a hovercraft comes into the sandbox with passengers on board to join the party. Agnes is extro-verting very markedly. She is acting in a young drama group and experimenting with her persona.

A golden ball has three colourful insects buzzing about nearby. In early Roman times a conception could be attributed to swallowing an insect; it equated to semen. Here Agnes' more conscious sexuality is hinted at again. A golden rose, or self-image, is at the bottom centre screened by two shells. Agnes was of Continental and British heritage, so the golden rose, the symbol of ancient European heritage, is very apt here. Her gifts in learning Italian and French suggest the Continental background of her mother as a valued potential. Above the rose is a golden turtle slowly ambling towards the dancing shells. Turtles combine a female round shell with a phallic male head. Its lubricity in general suggests a similarity to the female sexual organs. As the turtle carries its own armour in its shell-house there is a suggestion that Agnes' self-defence is now better established within her psychological life: self-confidence has strengthened her sense of poise and self-worth. She was now less shy, more outgoing, and determined. Becoming accustomed to her outstanding self-reliance gave her a firmer sense of who she was.

But the silver tree of life is overturning with 'high winds' from the left side of the sandbox. A yellow chick emerges from a many-coloured mystery stone (ovulation) and blue coloured shells and glass line the area. A quirky rabbit appears with a red bow-tie at the upper left hand corner, a caricature of the boys making awkward advances to her new-found sense of contained sexuality. Younger men are immature; older men are a mystery to Agnes now. The sand topography is roughened by the winds of change. The buffoons and the golden rose have not yet copulated within Agnes' psyche.

Sandplay 8

Combining many elements seen in earlier sandplays, the central hill (like the one in Sandplay 4) has a contained seed of wheat within a clear phallic tower (see Plate 31). A mirror is reflecting the silver tree of life upon which rests the dove, symbol of innocence and purity between the sky-heaven and the hill-earth. Two blue horses from Sandplay 2 go up towards the hilltop. The ring of dancing shells lies quietly at the base of the hill. To the lower right a stone within a pyramid suggests sharpening powers of awareness and incubation. Across the top, pagodas and flowering trees suggest the stages of growth and development the feminine must pass through and attain. At the upper left, a Chinese goddess serenely surveys the whole scene while near her feet two small dragons 'play' near the golden rose within its screen of two upstanding shells. A butterfly rests at the bottom left-hand corner representing transformation out of the cocoon into a resurrection from the egg and chrysalis to life's flight. Shakespeare has written, 'for men, like butterflies, sow not their wings but to the summer' (*Troilus and Cressida*, III, 3). It was late summer when this sandplay was made.

Robert Graves considered the butterfly able to fly crookedly but still to reach its goal. This may refer to Agnes' divorced household in which life flies 'crookedly' without a father living at home, but Agnes is reaching her goals of achievement at school and at home much more consistently now.

There is a sense at the top of the hill of impending growth mirrored back to Agnes' soul to prepare her for the powerful birth to come in her next sandplay.

Sandplay 9

The phallic sheath of wheat is lain down as the plinth on which the great white bull stands facing consciousness (see Plate 32). The bull, a solar and lunar animal, represents a powerful constellation of Agnes' animus, the contra-gender spiritual masculine force guarded by the Chinese wise man to its left and the Chinese wise woman to its right. The wheat is said to grow from the body of the bull in Mithraic cults – the bearer of the invisible god in Babylonia, Phoenicia, Egypt, and Palestine.

As lunar, the bull is sacrificed in Greek myth to Demeter, Venus, Urania, Athena and Hera. The white bull relates to the story of the moon goddess Pasiphae, who fell in love with a bull in her husband Minos' flock and seduced him with Daedalus' help by imitating a cow lying backwards. When the Minotaur was born of this union Minos hid him in the labyrinth for shame. In Egypt, whenever a new bull was installed in a temple, women exposed their genitals to him as a fertility rite.

In cosmogony, the white bull means chastity, patience and peace, which were qualities Agnes needed to handle her new vaginal power. Mithraic ritual used the bull to express the penetration of the feminine principle by the masculine.

To the upper right we have Kali who is always presaged in dreams and images by the white bull in Indian literature. Kali is the black mother, symbol here of the depressed mother to whom Agnes is devoted. Before Kali sits an Indian woman, symbol of the mistress of the father, always the 'personage' behind depression and loss for Agnes' mother psychologically. A mystical purple gate of the beyond stands high above these figures. In front of this pair, a small black girl and two white children look on like a distant memory of nursery, kindergarten, images of the child archetype and the real former childhood memories. Across on the lower left-hand corner is another manifestation of Agnes as a bejewelled Indian lady in blue, combing her very long hair. At the top left, an Indian man represents Agnes' father. He watches her protectively while playing the flute but she is faced away from him, away from her dark mother, and away from her father's lover. Her independence is flourishing.

Cows graze beneath the bull of animus, awaiting penetration and fecundation. Phallic towers mark the place of the bull.

Fully imaged, Agnes now has a powerful animus projection available to her psychological development. She takes her first trip abroad with a schoolfriend, not with her family. A ring of trees symbolize her growth and maturing stature.

Sandplay 10

In a moving final sandplay Agnes, as the central blue-dressed Indian lady, plays the drums across from her sister who joins in (see Plate 33). To the left her mother stands alone behind the seated lower couple, father and his second wife, playing instruments to inaugurate the extended family's dance of life. To the top right, Siva stands as Nataraja, the lord of the dance, with Parvati, 'daughter of the Himalayas' who is his wife, on the left. When Parvati dances the cosmic dance she becomes Kali and her dance, depicted in this sandplay, unfolds on the plane of the human soul. She dances in this manifestation of Kali to the music of Agnes' family as Indians, to remove sin, weakness and attachment from all who are present. Then true identity may be formed again by all concerned.

In the lower right-hand corner, three vessels of containment stand, representing Agnes, her mother and sister as the family of three women. In Agnes' clay pot sand is put, a symbol of the healing transformation Agnes has experienced in sandplay. Her *rite de passage* to young womanhood is one of the telling examples of how sandplay can help a young person to reach towards maturity under the stress of first menstruation at the very time of her parents' divorce.

88

At the top, two water-buffalo, symbols of strength and mutuality-as-pain stand near Sive and Parvati, the beautiful couple onto whom Agnes projects her hope for union one day to her very own 'god-man'.

Sandplay heals where stress and development is most pointed. Its non-verbal power enabled an originally focused but shy young woman to experience before her very eyes and in the presence of a sustaining male therapist, the very essence of entering woman-hood. Sandplay excludes embarrassment, apology or dissembling. Its images to those initiated to its synthetic interpretation help *nature itself to explore itself.*

Where sandplay interpretation is 'adultomorphic' it is so deliberately as it inspires and stretches the imagination of those schooled only to rationality, discipline and hard work. Its free but firm grounding to transitory anxieties give it a holding power enabling nature itself to better take its course. I am indebted to Agnes and her parents for the release of this case as a tool for educational psychology in the Jungian tradition.

THE SYNTHETIC METHOD OF INTERPRETATION

In concluding these four clinical cases, I would like to defend Jung's theory of synthetic interpretation which I have used throughout.

Unlike reductive methods which try to trace everything back to primitive instincts, in the interpretation of Jungian sandplay the synthetic method develops the material into a process for differentiating the material. Thus the synthetic method elaborates symbolic fantasy within sandplay. This entails an introversion of libido, sacrificing a former attitude towards a new one when image interpretation reveals what this new attitude can be. The transition to a new attitude was termed by Jung as the 'transcendent function'.

Concepts become metaphorical in symbology when we shed light on their possible meanings. Sandplay in its creativity neither knows nor possesses these meanings absolutely; what symbolic interpretation does is raise possibilities that strengthen the patient's ego and raise its differentiation further from unconsciousness. Ideas, in sandplay construction, emerge as acts of conscious differentiation from an unconscious source. The ego then considers the interpretation revealed and can reunite with the self, as did primitive man in his *participation mystique* with nature.

Where psyche is a living experience in sandplay, the idea does not petrify but gets visible three-dimensional expression by the sandplayer quite literally in front of their eyes. This produces a new potential: after identifying with sandplays that may return to archaic collective material of regress to the psychic conditions of prehistory, the retrograde process is renewed by here-and-now consciousness of its relative meanings for the self of the sandplayer. This impressive experience seems to renew the psyche's ongoing dynamic state.

Where a submersion to instinct occurs, resistance to its dynamic chaos is compensated by a need for form and order. Sandplay enables a fast and flexible shift between the chaos–order dimension. The psyche of the sandplayer creates the symbol that expresses this dynamic spectrum which frees libido bound into the unconscious. A release from the bondage of trapped energies is what the symbol always tries to point to and partially elucidate. The images of childhood fantasies and the later projection of the child archetype in its conscious images strive for fulfilment and integration in the adult when using sandplay. Fantasy often foretells of events foreshadowed in the unconscious.

Jung remarked more than once that a *redeeming symbol comes from the place where no one expects it*. Lack of prior assumptions is the most important attitude when building a sandplay. Symbolic play is a middle way in which opposites can flow together in a new movement. Functions that were inert tend to come to life; the repressed and undervalued elements come into sandplay through the least valued function of conscious life. A restriction of the total potential of the sandplayer is what is stimulated through sandplay. The blocked psyche flows again away from the lure of a maternal abyss. New blossoming life overgrows the aridity as in Isaiah:

> Then shall the eyes of the blind be opened, and the ears of the deaf shall be unstopped.
> Then shall the lame man leap up as an hart, and the tongue of the dumb sing: for in the wilderness shall waters break out, and streams in the desert.
>
> (Isaiah 35:5)

5

PASSING BY THE AUTHOR'S STUDY ROOM

THE FIRST MAPPING OF SANDPLAY FORMS

There has tended to be a tacit agreement among most of my sandplay colleagues not to 'map' the areas of the sandtrays pertaining to areas of psyche being projected. This is a too easy refusal to discuss the difficulties of observing tendencies which occur over great numbers of sandplays. Because of the number of variables involved it is not an easy matter to envisage statistical proof. I took 1000 sandplays at random and got 95 per cent or more showing the following tendencies in design which the diagrams to follow capture pictorially. I believe they are a helpful guide as to what probably will happen in most sandplay processes. There will remain many unique exceptions, of course, which is why sandplay is so endlessly fascinating.

There are three principal levels of psyche being projected into sandplays: the conscious level, the level of the personal unconscious and the level of the collective (archetypal) unconscious. This gives seven basic combinations of level, some or all of which may be possible to any one diagram. I shall number each one as set out below and then indicate in discussing each diagram which levels could be present within it.

Levels of projection in sandplay

Level 1. Conscious only.
Level 2. Personal unconscious only.
Level 3. Collective unconscious only.
Level 4. Conscious plus personal unconscious.
Level 5. Conscious plus collective unconscious.

Level 6. Personal unconscious plus collective unconscious.
Level 7. Conscious plus both personal and collective unconscious.
(Level 7 very often describes the levels present in an adult's first
    sandplay.)

In presenting the diagrams below I am attempting to indicate the
tendency which the psyche takes in creating original and spontaneous sandplays. There is no sense in which these diagrams take
any formal order, rule or theory. In my search for the hidden forms
the psyche utilizes in sandplay, these diagrams express a form
present 950 times out of 1000 in a random sampling from my adult
patients' archives of sandplay photographs.

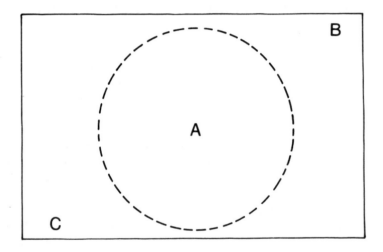

Figure 5.1

Figure 5.1 shows the most usual order in which sandplayers
choose to build a topography. Of course there are sandplays where
the surface of the sand is not changed. Here we are only interested
in those sandplays where the sand is modelled or moved about.
Generally a sandplayer will build or change the central area (A),
then move on to the upper right (B) and then the lower left (C). The
majority way of moulding the sand I have come to name the
'Classical' approach. Levels 2, 3, 4, 5, 6 or 7 as defined above may
be present in projection of psyche here.

In Figure 5.2 we have an approximation of areas when ego
material is most likely to be expressed and where archetypal

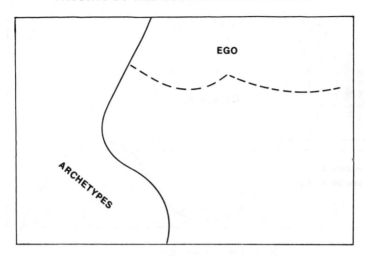

EGO

ARCHETYPES

Figure 5.2

material most often occurs. There are sandplays, of course, where all of the box is ego-level or all is archetypal as I have indicated in the Levels list. When it was broken up, however, this was the pattern that emerged 95 per cent of the time in adult patients. Levels 5 or 7 apply to this diagram.

Figure 5.3 refers to the placement of objects only in relation to body movement, decision to have the object so placed and the sense of deliberateness in so doing. The upper half of the sandbox received a more deliberate attitude from sandplayers than did the lower half of the sandbox. Here Levels 1, 2, 3, 4 or 5 apply.

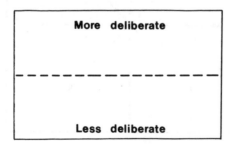

More deliberate

Less deliberate

Figure 5.3

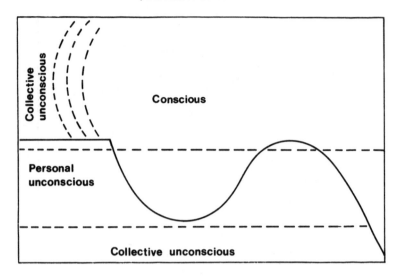

Figure 5.4

In sandplays using Levels 4, 5 or 7 we get this intriguing interplay of the interfaces between conscious material, personal unconscious projection and the images of the collective unconscious (Figure 5.4). This design when these Levels are present is one of the most powerfully present of my different categories showing often occurring tendencies.

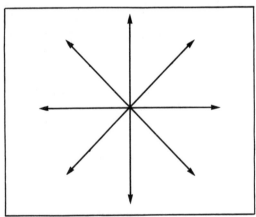

Figure 5.5

94

Figure 5.5 relates to relativities in the sandplayers' material. The arrows can refer to relations of direction, complementarity, direct opposites, complementary opposites, colour balances in the objects chosen or lines of dynamic movement in 'active' objects indicating action. Levels 1, 2, 3, 4, 5, 6 or 7 apply to this schema.

Figure 5.6

Relating only to Levels 2, 3 or 6 the 'doubles as defence' (Figure 5.6) show designs in topography or use of objects where two lines are used like battlements or defend psychic material. The defensive mandala has been widely discussed in Jungian literature and would apply here. There tends to be a more angular design in the right side corners than in the left very often. It is a mistake to assume a double-design mandala is necessarily a manifestation of the self: it may only indicate a besieged and troubled ego problematic.

In Levels 2, 3, 4, 5, 6 or 7 we often see that the anima and sometimes the animus will take images in the upper left-hand corner of the sandplay (Figure 5.7). Family constellations often occur in the lower right-hand corner, along with masculine or anima constellations more rarely. I tend in a full process always to get anima and animus material in developmental images of great

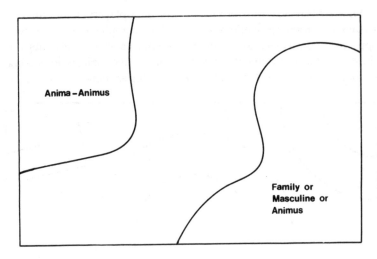

Figure 5.7

power. The sandplay is one of the best proofs of Jung's archetypal theory in this regard that we have.

True manifestations of the self may occur at all Levels – 1, 2, 3, 4, 5, 6 or 7. I find the dynamic action with or against the self more

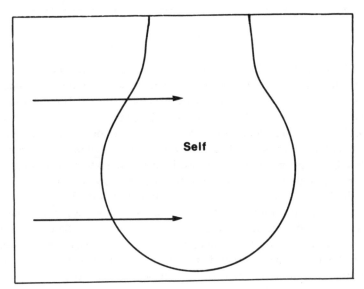

Figure 5.8

often emanates from the left side, if it is expressed (Figure 5.8). The general central position of self is most often found, not in only a circular shape but in a more sphere-like area that may not be tightly marked in the sand.

These eight diagrams indicate some of the principal mappings I have found to be significant. There are myriads of others; I claim these to be one indication of certain universal tendencies that occur in my adult patients. We cannot control the atmosphere, size, colour or shape of professional sandplay rooms which may outwardly affect – as does the therapist's personality – all that happens inwardly as patients make their sandplays. Measurement is probably impossible; hints and glimpses, however, can be given through these maps of tendencies present in sandplayers' psyche.

SANDPLAY AS DIAGNOSTIC

I have indicated that the general mapping studies above have too many uncontrollable variables to be suitable to statistical verification. At a recent annual conference of the International Society for Sandplay Therapy (Founder: Dora Kalff), hosted by the British Branch and chaired in London by the author, a group of four members from Milan gave a paper entitled 'The Use of Sandplay Therapy in the Psychiatric Service of a Pediatric Hospital' that foreshadows the possible use of statistical proofs with sandplay. The authors who are Jungian analysts are S. Marinucci, F. Montecchi, G. Nagliero and D. Tortolani. This team has been able to begin to describe differences in the sandplays of children who have cancer, determining who is likely to live and who is likely to die. They have the facilities at the Bambino Gesu Hospital for psychotherapeutic sandplay work in which they record much that happens in a session; verbal and non-verbal behaviour, choices and use of the materials, how used and in which order the objects are placed in the sandbox. The sandplay is photographed and using notes and drawings the therapist can elaborate a diagnosis considering components such as:

1   the use of sand and the sandbox
2   the choice of objects
3   the actual construction
4   the use of space
5   the verbalization and the non-verbal behaviour.

With cancer patients, it was found that prognostic indications about the evolution of the tumour pathology could be discovered from the initial sandplays of oncological patients. This created a possibility to change the rigid, pre-established bio-psychological programme, which limits so severely the patient's quality of life. Carcinogenesis and its relation to affectivity and stress have suggested that the general characteristics of persons with cancer are: a difficulty in elaborating affective losses, a depressive and desperate temperament, an inability to accept and deal with aggressive tendencies, a preference for negation and removal as a defence mechanism, and difficulty in symbolization. With children who have cancer there is a tendency not to request enough parental care and massive behavioural regression may result.

Four children with tumours made sandplays and their work was described. An 11-year-old boy had a kidney tumour. He was not tolerating his therapy and had been referred to sandplay. He made a very complex scene, constructed clockwise, beginning in the lower right-hand corner and finishing, with a small forest, in the upper right-hand corner. He described the scene himself as follows:

> The cowboys are attacking the Indians as they want to take possession of their territory and animals; here are some squaws who are giving birth to their children. Here is a forest with animals searching for prey and here, on a rocky peak, are an eagle and some coyotes waiting for the end of the battle so they and their offspring can feed on the dead. And here is a sow nursing her litter.

It is evident in his sandplay that this boy represents violence, with archaic oral aggressive valences, together with soft, delicate details. It is a very dynamic scene in which birth, death and rebirth are presented all together and circularly connected in a continuous transformation.

A 12-year-old girl with a Wilms tumour was referred because she refused the prescribed therapy which could cause the loss of her hair. She was fond of her hair and asked her mother to comb it constantly. She spent a good part of the session smoothing and patting the wet sand, making small furrows as streets, placing and then rearranging in an obsessive way the materials in the sandbox. She constructed a small town where everything is calm and in perfect order; everyone is in his place. 'More than anything,' she said, 'there is no confusion ... I hate confusion ... it's a place where

I would like to live; in fact, it seems to be the town where I live.'

This girl repeated this scene almost identically in the next two sessions, constructing it in the same way and making analogous comments. In the third session she refused to construct another sandplay.

Everything in this sandplay was fixed and immobile in time and space. The way it was constructed shows a preference to negate and remove any aggressive impulse or any 'shadow' whatsoever. It seemed that the prime concern was to fossilize time and space.

An 11-year-old boy with a rabdomyosarcoma refused the limitations the doctors imposed; he would sneak off to play football in spite of the fact that part of his chest had been resected.

He assembled a forest in which various animals and a hunter roamed about looking for prey. His comment was: 'It's an ecological scene, there are many aggressive animals but there is no reason to be afraid because they kill only for survival; it's a question of equilibrium.' The second session gave prognostic indications. The scene presents a modern man among a group of fighting dinosaurs and he explains that:

> Charlie Chaplin was playing with a time-machine and found himself in prehistory when dinosaurs ate each other and man lived on raw meat. If I were in such a situation I wouldn't know what to do because I don't know how people lived in those days.

To a question as to what happens next he replied, 'Charlie was so shocked by the scene that, with the help of an expert, he returned to his times, never again to play with a time machine.' The characteristics of this scene are orality, primitive aggression and a disturbed perception of time that projects the boy into prehistory beyond the personal story. However, the boy does not falter – just as in real life he refuses to give up quality.

The first picture of another 11-year-old boy who had embryonic rabdomyosarcoma was requested because he refused his prescribed therapy. With each antiblastic application he complained of lacerating pain in his legs that had no medical explanation. His father complained that, in reality, this therapy only worsened his son's condition. In fact, his father carried him to each session as he did not walk. Not long after the beginning of this intense pain both the psychiatric and oncological interventions were interrupted as the boy refused to leave his home.

The boy's descriptive comment about his sandplay was as follows:

It is a peaceful farm where they have everything they need. Their only worry is to keep the wolves on the other side of the river. At one time several wolves attacked the farmer but did not kill him; however, they did eat a sheep. Everything is at a standstill. The tractor is placed in front of the gate making it difficult to pass through.

When the therapist indicated the bridges and a shepherd who seemed to be going out the boy replied: 'The shepherd wants to take the sheep out but the father is afraid and tells him not to go. The shepherd thinks there is more grass on the other side of the river but is returning to the farm.' After a long pause he concluded: 'It seems like my grandparents' farm. That was a nice place and when I was little I liked to go there.' It is worth mentioning that three of this boy's grandparents had died of cancer and that his father had had a serious invalidating nephropathy.

In this picture, as in the others, there is a clear attempt to fix time and a happy place, eliminating every possible aggressive valence, but the price is to stop living. Here too, time is not his time and places are not his places, but both time and place are those of his father and his grandparents.

Some two and a half years after these sandplays were made, the first and third patients were 'cured', the second and fourth died several months after the sandplay interventions. There are many implications, some of which I will briefly list here:

1   the disturbance of the psychological dimension of time
2   the permanence/fixation at an archaic oral stage
3   the patients' relation with their aggressive impulses and their shadows in general
4   the role of parental fantasies and the container/content interplay between parent and child
5   contact with the construction of the individual self and its relation with time.

The analysts from Milan pointed out that the patients, at least thus far at the clinic, who have come through the tunnel of cancer are those who were able to represent and confront their oral aggressive valences without denying them. These patients still have a whole self including the terrifying experience of an archetypal shadow.

They still have the possibility to deal with their psychic impulses: to accept them, to contain them, to transform them and give them a meaning.

In reference to time, another boy patient remarked, 'the past always tried to return and to destroy the present because it does not realize that things change and that some things do not return'. The primary need of these patients is to be supported in their struggle, to be helped to keep hope alive in spite of the horror they are living. They have not given up on life, they need help to stay alive.

The situation of the two patients who died was quite different. Either they had never been in contact with the self or it was earlier irreparably damaged; its substitute is a primordial fantasy of an Eden and it is necessary to keep away every aggressive impulse or any transforming event from this Eden. Time and space are fossilized in a dimension without history; if they do have a history it is that of their parents and they cannot separate from it. This is why they have given up on life, and perhaps they are simply asking to be helped to die.

The Milan sandplay therapists point out that the doomed children have no history consciously of themselves as separate from their parents. The critical identification of self is described in Chapter 2 in the discussion of Winnicott's theory of the 'transitional object'. For these children this phase has not occurred and separation, when attempted through illness, goes all the way into physical death with such children. The implications of this fact have yet to register with most social services, paediatric hospitals and nursery schools. If those helping children were more aware of the implications, more helpful and preventive interventions could be taken.

It would appear from the way this team is working in Milan that it may be possible to get some acceptable hard statistical facts drawn from the sandplays of tumour patients and that sufficient control of the variable-problem may be possible to devise enabling statistical proofs to be elaborated over time. This would take away some of the suspicion in academic psychology circles that depth psychologists make fanciful interpretations. The diagnostic future of sandplay is just being born.

FREE-WHEELING USES OF SANDPLAY

There is a form of sandplay intervention which should be used only by very experienced intuitives. I have observed Dora Kalff using this technique and, after years of experience in the formal use of sandplay, I have used it twice: once at a Buddhist college during a special course when Mrs Kalff became ill and I substituted for her and a second time in the hills above Adelaide, Australia, at a distinguished healing centre. This use of sandplay is all the things analysis is not: it is predictive soothsaying as astrology is and it can be most effective. Only one sandplay is made. It is interpreted immediately as fully as possible.

Although it might seem surprising, some remarkable healing and insight has been gained by some of these one-off sandplayers but I would caution that this is not a method, but a special intuitive reading of one sandplay. In the hands of a very perceptive practitioner it can have helpful and even valuable psychological results for the maker of a sandplay.

Another variation in the work with children is the participation of the therapist in making the sandplay with the child. This usually involves some verbal feedback to know what is happening between child and therapist; my objection is not to the occasional use of words but to the defences in a child that will be called up if the adult therapist makes interventions by playing with the child. This technique is endangered by the authoritarian fears children have of adults and by the manipulation and persuasion of the therapist. I believe it is when a child goes free of adult immediate response, that they can express spontaneously, without interruption or curtailment, the heartfelt needs, problems, feelings, wishes and fears directly into the sandplay. Concentration is much deeper when a free and protected space is offered. The 'conversational' aspect of a therapist playing with the child is just what the child needs release from, because of difficult or adverse situations at home or school. The child doesn't want a guessing game such as what move the therapist will make next in constructing the scene. That is too much like the daily struggle of young children with the adult world.

The exception to this is work with autistic children where connections of all kinds are in jeopardy. A 'mirroring' set of construction moving with the autistic child's construction may give such a child a glimpse of relatedness or of meaning which needs the interaction and participation of the therapist directly. Certain problems might be relieved or solved if situations in the sandplay are mutually overcome by the autistic child and by the therapist building co-laterally in an atmosphere that is quiet and unforced. Where possible, I have found it beneficial to the autistic to help them gradually to gain the independent use of the sandbox by slowly withdrawing the therapist's direct intervention while remaining sitting closer to the sandbox than one would with a normal child.

While the use of sandplay for children has mushroomed into use at psychiatric day centres, in establishing child abuse in courts of law, with the autistic and the physically handicapped, what further possibilities are there for the use of sandplay with adults, by trained sandplay therapists, outside the consulting room?

As a deep reciprocal therapy involving process, transference and insightful delayed interpretation, I believe there is no acceptable alternative method to a Jungian archetypal and symbolic setting to sandplay and working through of the sandplayer's material in a series of sandplays that trace and reveal developmental process.

However, experiments are going on with group procedures. One, in California, involves a group who meet and one member volunteers to make a sandplay; then, led by a sandplay therapist, the remainder of the group comment upon the sandplay as well and jostle the ideas and images about.

What I question here is the possibility of a performance element creeping in when a sandplay is made in front of and partly for a group. Knowing the mixed scrutiny that is to come puts a sandplayer into very many pressures of conscious adaptation which may block the release of unconscious material. The point of the work may become eroded and a game of charades may result: the sandplay-maker may be only pretending and less concentrated in a group and the interpretive intervention of the group may have little more than a crowd response to the sandplay.

It has been suggested that factories and offices should have sandplay rooms for use at break-times. The danger here is that the unconscious material unleashed in a sandplay might unwittingly cause someone an industrial accident afterwards or other disturbing aftermath experiences. Where a sandplay is uncontained by a therapist and the therapist's sandplay room as the place of ritual, the danger of unlocking psychosis under no control or holding situation, rules out in my mind the use of free, unmonitored sandplay in industry or the professions. While this is a pity, psyche in our time is so troubled and often so borderline as to preclude the free-wheeling self-interpretive use of the medium.

Sexual images are often very graphic in sandplay. Usually made unconsciously in the hills and valleys of topography, breasts and vaginas, penises, testicles and anuses emerge often enough for interpretation and integration. I recall once a man who made a complicated set of mountains, ridges and valleys and then realized a hand was masturbating a penis in the scenery. This led to other related associations and a breakthrough in the therapeutic work. In the first case I describe in Chapter 4, the sandplay where a uterus was made by a male patient had a breakthrough effect on that case on many levels at once.

The earth quality of sand pulls the psyche towards body expression and this can be of inestimable value to the therapy.

The use of colour in the objects placed in the sandbox needs a research book in itself to be elucidated. I would mention briefly that complementarity in vivid colours chosen or pastel colours chosen can have a linking effect between objects that requires interpretation. The use of alchemical colours – black, white, red, green or gold – must be carefully analysed and often earth colours – the browns, dark reds, beiges, greys, whites and blacks – will be used by patients for special meanings and levels of unconscious expression. Primary colours may be exclusively used as archetypal givens, and Steiner's colour theories fit well together with Jung's basic functional colours into interpretation. These theories are well documented by their authors and need careful study before a therapist applies them to sandplay interpretation.

I have often been asked when lecturing if the sandplay medium can contain spiritual and religious expression. To the same extent as dreams will, the 'awake dream' of sandplay creation often contains a rich and varied working through of a patient's spiritual/religious dilemma. Many objects representing gods and goddesses are available together with shrines, retreats, churches, temples, cathedrals and chapels. These figures and buildings can be used to help the living through of various forms of inner marriages in psyche involving diverse concepts and spiritual images. Both Eastern and Western symbolic figures are available to express the invaluable aspect of individuation within the sandplay process. Many agnostics and atheists have discovered through sandplay the unconscious release of integrative archetypal material which consciously enables them to contact the God-image within their own psyche. This was the last thing they expected but the challenge and witness of the sandplay material was there for them to interpret and begin to live with in a new way.

Reconnection to childhood in sandplay through memories of childhood holidays at the beach or playing in a sandpit at home or at school can help an adult sandplayer begin to regress sufficiently to construct childhood scenes where archetypal images can assist in reinterpreting what happened as psychological fact, not just so-called historical fact. Atmospheres of childhood are more non-verbal in memory than adult life usually is and the medium of sand can sometimes release more quickly the hidden, repressed content of early memory and begin to reconstruct the past. This synthesizes past with present towards future. Sandplay facilitates the return of early memory and can lead on to valuable work in the reconstruction and repair of a traumatic childhood.

I have repeatedly observed that sandplayers return after a first process, often after a few years have elapsed, and want to do another series. This return to a continuing effort towards further self-knowing can unleash a series of sandplays even more revealing at a conscious level than before. Often favourite objects from the first series are used in new ways. The 'story' in psyche continues. With resistances almost totally dropped through acquaintance with the sandplay experience, the manifestation of the self is often more clarified and revealed than in an initial process. Psyche is tireless in its variety and its apparently endless possibility for expression.

THE UNIVERSALITY OF SANDPLAY

The outstanding attribute of sandplay therapy which ensures its future is its universality. It requires no technique of any kind to mould sand into a world topography or to place objects into the sandbox which can easily be changed within the session (unlike painting and clay modelling where, once the paint or clay dries, it is much more difficult and frustrating to make changes). Free of language restraints, sandplay is open to patients of any age. Verbal therapy requires a considerable language base even in child analysis and in adult analysis cultural background – social, political and religious – has to be considered in relation to the analytical situation.

There is a surprising sense of freedom in sandplay that many patients have trouble finding in free association with words. The sense of *overview* in making a sandplay gives insights spontaneously that few patients make using language early on in a process, unless they are adept at lateral thinking.

The visual image of the finalized sandplay is using that power of vision with which we most *receive* the world. To *conceive* a sandplay is to use that mode closest to our perceiving mental organization, the three-dimensional visual world, a factor of central importance and influence for the unconscious and the conscious to utilize. In actively using the hands to build the sandplay there is a sense of craft involved which is spontaneous and leads the mind on its expression of the psychological situation. The single-mindedness of a sandplayer working without interference, discussion or interruption from the therapist – but knowing the therapist is there as observer – holds an influence of direct expressiveness in many sandplays which clarifies the position of the patient's psyche to a startling degree of flow and revelation of process. The image is photographed and the record of the psychic material held for symbolic and dynamic interpretation. One of therapy's most powerful tools, sandplay stands alone for its inspiration towards, and alignment with, archetypal and personal projections of a differentiation that is outstanding among the projective therapies. A healing therapy of diagnostic and psychotherapeutic excellence, sandplay is indeed a wonderful therapy.

Dora Kalff (1980) has pointed out that the course of psychic development might be compared with flowing water. Hexagram 29 (K'an/The Abysmal (Water)) of the *I Ching* says:

> It flows on and on, merely filling at the place it traverses; it does not shy away from any dangerous place, nor from any sudden plunge; nothing can make it lose its own intrinsic essence. It remains true to itself in all circumstances. Thus, truthfulness in difficult conditions will bring about the penetration of a situation within one's heart. And once a situation is mastered from within the heart, the success of our exterior actions will come about all by itself.
>
> (Wilhelm 1951, p. 115)

When we succeed with a Jungian analysis that has been aided by the unconscious projections within sandplays we can speak of good fortune, effective interpretive work, and the grace of God.

EPILOGUE

Fierce storms had overwhelmed the Zürich lakeshore throughout the winter days of 1990 I spent lecturing at the Jung Institute in Küssnacht. With the lectures behind me, my wife and I went to lunch at an ancient Swiss farmhouse at the edge of the next Zürich suburb. I rang the ancient house bell. I noticed the date inscribed over the front door. It was 1485.

We had come to lunch with Martin and Sabina Kalff in the house of sandplay for the first time since Dora Kalff's death. Her son and daughter-in-law greeted us warmly through their sadness. We were full of talk about the time of Dora's passing, her gradual decline, and her peaceful acceptance of the approach to death.

Then we descended the old steps to the sandplay rooms on the lower ground floor. I entered the oldest sandplay room where I had undertaken my sandplay with Dora Kalff twenty years before. The room was strangely still.

Martin wanted to give me one of his mother's pieces from her great sandplay collection of miniature objects. I chose a Japanese gate signifying entrance to a spiritual place. There were several such gates exactly the same, so removing one didn't alter the look of the shelf at all. It seemed as if it had always been mine.

I took it as we went to Dora's grave and I wanted to place it in a niche above the grave site in the sunlight just for a moment. Unconsciously I put it upside down in the niche.

We are living in an upside-down world. It is the dead who are the right side up.

The glorious flowers on the tomb spoke to me of my time of study and assimilation and the long years of clinical experience using sandplay in my practice in London.

The late afternoon shadows fell as we walked back to the house, the international archive of our sandplay group. My wife and I returned to our lakeside hotel and quietly walked by the water's edge as the sun set. We would soon be walking into the sunset of life ourselves. We were in a spiritual silence as calm was restored to the silvery lake's surface after long days of violent storm waves.

Thank you, Dora Kalff, for giving me an understanding of the most powerful psychological therapy now available in the world – Jungian Sandplay, the Wonderful Therapy.

BASIC SANDPLAY
EQUIPMENT

Sandplay room
A special room is provided for sandplay separate from the verbal analytic consulting room.

Sandtray
A specially built sandbox, approximately 18 inches deep by 23 inches across by 3½ inches high, of which the sides and interior bottom are waterproofed and painted in the colour of azure blue water. The sandtray is placed on a low table and filled with sand to about one-half the depth of the tray. One dry sandtray and one wet sandtray are provided for free choice. Miniature figures are displayed on shelves on the walls of the sandplay room.

Water jugs are available to add water for moulding the sand if needed.

Figures and objects representing the 'world'
Small toy-sized miniatures representing human, animal, plant and mineral life are presented. Buildings for all purposes are provided from as many cultures as possible. Prehistoric and fantasy animals are available. Cultural, historic and symbolic figures from East and West are provided. Vehicles of land, sea and air are included.

Sandplay slides
Kodachrome colour slides record the patient's series of sandplays. Photos are taken after the patient leaves the session before the sandplay is dismantled by the therapist.

GUIDELINES FOR TRAINING TO BECOME A SANDPLAY THERAPIST

Aims of the training

As a result of the training one will be accepted into the International Society for Sandplay Therapy. On the basis of this membership one is entitled to use 'Sandplay' in the way established by its founder, Dora Kalff.

The training is understood as a supplementary training.

Qualifications for training

Applicants for training are expected to show evidence of having the following qualifications:

1 A university education as a medical doctor, pedagogue, psychologist, theologian, clinical social worker, or a specialized training in one of the humanities or social sciences. Persons not having a university education but who can demonstrate adequate educational background will also be considered.
2 Some knowledge of psychopathology, psychodiagnosis and psychotherapy, which shall preferably have been achieved by formal study and applied clinical experience with patients/ clients.
3 Evidence of having had some in-depth inner development and insight such as may be achieved in the experience of personal analysis, meditation or other disciplines leading to such developments.
4 Licensure to practise psychotherapy in countries and regions where licensure is required.

Exceptions will be made for exceptional persons.

Course of training

Personal experience

The experience of the Sandplay process on a personal basis under the guidance of a qualified Sandplay therapist is fundamental and required. This should lead to an experience of the particular possibilities of Sandplay for helping to unfold one's own self-realization.

If possible, the personal Sandplay experience should precede a regular attendance at seminars on Sandplay in order to safeguard the spontaneous character of this experience.

Theoretical training

Theoretical training in the practice of Sandplay is principally derived from individual study and participation in training seminars. The relationship of the Sandplay process to the general history of the evolution of consciousness as it is expressed in religions, mythologies and the traditions of various cultures will be studied.

During this phase of the training three theoretical seminar papers are required. In these papers elements of the work with Sandplay should be connected with research in psychology and other fields.

Practicum and supervision

Practical work with patients/clients during training will be regularly supervised in individual and group sessions. At the conclusion of training one completed case will be formally presented to the training committee for review and determination of qualification for membership.

For information write to Joel Ryce-Menuhin, 85 Canfield Gardens, London NW6 3EA, UK.

THE LOWENFELD–KALFF CORRESPONDENCE

Margaret Lowenfeld in her important pioneering work in London with 'World Pictures' in the sand kept in touch with Dora Kalff and their correspondence in the 1950s and 1960s, which I have carefully studied in full from the Lowenfeld Archives, shows mutual respect. Otherwise, it is an unexpectedly uneventful exchange of very polite circumambulations. Here is an example of an exchange about the interpretation of a horse symbol to which Kalff did not reply showing how frustrating it is for an archivist in sandplay when all issues are avoided.

June 2nd, 1957

Dear Dr Lowenfeld,

Some time ago I have sent you my paper on my experience with the world pictures. As I told you, it is the only copy and I would be glad to have it back. Do you think that it is possible to send it to me? I would be very happy if you would say a word on it. But I am sure that you are very busy as always. Maybe that I come to London between short trips and in that case I would be looking forward very much to visit you and your clinic.

With all best wishes and kind regards.

Sincerely yours,
Dora M. Kalff.

26th June, 1957

Dear Mrs Kalff,

I was very glad to get your letter and I want first to apologize very much indeed for having kept your Manuscript all this time. It is really very good of you to have allowed me to have your only

112

copy and I appreciate it very much. I have kept it carefully and am now returning it thoughtfully.

The reason why I have kept it so long is concerned with my book on the World Technique. I am very interested in your paper, it is the only thesis that I have seen which presents the World Technique in a Jungian background, and I have been turning over in my mind both your paper in itself and its relation to the whole presentation of the World Technique. I like your paper. I think it makes a very good presentation of the value of the World apparatus and I am particularly interested in the fact that you find, as I do, that it proves so valuable an instrument also in the treatment of adults. Two points only in your paper I would like to discuss with you at some time – I have put a pencil cross in the margin beside them. These are your treatment of the horse as a feminine symbol and what you say about the circus. Take the horse first. I am very glad to hear that you may be coming to London and I would like, if it were possible, to arrange a small discussion with you on the use of the World with adults, if this were possible. The difficulty is one of time. June and July are impossible months in London as all the Societies have long conferences and it makes the timetable extremely crowded, so I would be glad to know as long beforehand as possible, supposing you do come, what dates you will be here and what evening would be possible for you. The horse from our point of view is practically always either an instinct (E) symbol or a masculine one and I would be most interested to know why you felt that this particular horse was feminine.

Secondly, about the circus. Our children constantly make use of the circus figures and it is very rare to find them aware of the side of circus performers you interpret here. To the English child it seems to me a circus is much more a strange kind of grown-up play, exciting and marvellous, and in most cases we find it associated with the bewildered excitement aroused in children by any contact with adult sexuality. I think our workers at the I.C.P. would like to discuss this with you. But to come back to the thesis itself. I would very much like to have a copy of this in our Library. Would it be possible for you to have a copy made? Quite a number of our workers read German and our senior workers particularly I think would be very interested to read it. If you could at any time achieve an English translation this would also be valuable and I would particularly like to have a translation of your last two pages. I am considering including these in the book on the technique. We have a

113

chapter dealing with the experiences of other workers while using the technique, and it is here that it would be included.

Are you in touch with the Society for Analytical Psychology or with the club of Jungians in London and do you know the London situation at all? It is unfortunately a very tangled one owing to conflicting interests and conflicting ideas, particularly between those trained in Zürich who come to England as already practising analysts and those who have been trained in England only. This situation makes it always delicate and difficult for anyone who is not a Jungian, to move with any certainty with the Jungians in London, and one needs always to know before one does know exactly what the relationships are, so if you could write me about this it would be a help.

Thank you for sending me the photographs. I find these difficult to see being small but probably they come out in much better detail when projected on a screen. Would it be possible for you to bring your collection of World photographs with you and I would try to see if I can borrow a projector here with which perhaps, if there were an opportunity, you could demonstrate them at I.C.P.

With kind regards,

Yours sincerely,
Margaret Lowenfeld

Enc.

Several times later in the correspondence there were suggested meetings or conference invitations which never came off. Every time Mrs Kalff sent a pupil to London, the contact with Dr Lowenfeld didn't work for unexplained reasons. The letters between Lowenfeld and Kalff were always cordial and expressed interests that seemed more diplomatic than professionally interesting. They asked about each other's work and then kept on going on their very separate ways.

It was Kalff who brought the Jungian background to sandplay. Although several gifted pupils of Lowenfeld have always claimed that Lowenfeld was not really Freudian (and I can agree from her excellent books that there may have been eclectic tendencies), Lowenfeld was not Jungian in the sense we think of it in London in the 1990s. For me, she was iconoclastic yet creative in her remarkable work *The World Technique* (1977), in a basically Freudian setting and Zeitgeist. Lowenfeld had wide interests and knew the professional London Jungian scene well in a friendly collegial manner.

In originating the term 'sandplay', Dora Kalff correctly got Lowenfeld's permission to differentiate the Jungian work from the 'World Technique', and to separate herself out and away from Lowenfeld from then onwards. Pioneers are usually polite to each other as they steadfastly go on their individual paths. Pioneers are also, by definition, ego-centric if not 'ego-eccentric'!

NOTE ON
RYCE-MENUHIN'S
BRITISH SANDPLAY
GROUP

The British Branch of the International Society for Sandplay Therapy (Founder: Dora Kalff) was founded by Joel Ryce-Menuhin, B.Mus., B.Sc., M.Phil., IGAP, IAAP in January 1988. Its Honorary Patrons are Baroness Vera von der Heydt, IGAP, IAAP; Sir Yehudi and Lady Menuhin, O.M., K.B.E.; Geoffrey Carton; Fiona Leyland; Roberto and Eila Hershon-Guerra; Ruth Lazarus; Dr Dagmar Leichti von Brasch M.D.; Dr Roderick M. Peters, M.B., M.R.C.P., M.Sc., SAP, IAAP; Yaltah Menuhin Ryce; Johannes Wasmuth; and, *in memoriam*: Cecil E. Burney, Ph.D; Dr Violet de Laszlo, SGIAP, IAAP; and Helen Dowling.

REFERENCES

Adler, G. (1966) *Studies in Analytical Psychology* (2nd edn), New York: G.P. Putnam's Sons, p. 122.

—— (1979) 'Ego integration and patterns of the coniunctio' in *Dynamics of the Self*, London: Coventure.

Bastian, A. (1860) *Der Mensch in der Geschichte*, Leipzig: Wigand.

Boëhme, J. (1934) *The Signature of All Things, with Other Writings* (trans. W. Law), London: J.M. Dent and Sons (first published in 1682).

Bradway, K. (1985) *Sandplay Bridges and Transcendent Function*, San Francisco: C.G. Jung Books.

Budge, E.A.W. (1960) *The Book of the Dead*, New York: University Books.

Coomaraswamy, A.K. (1977) *Selected Papers*, vol. 2 Bollingen Series LXXXIX, Princeton: University Press.

de Vries, A. (1984) *Dictionary of Symbols and Imagery*, Amsterdam: Elsevier Science Publishers.

Eliade, M. (1958) *Yoga: Immortality and Freedom*, Bollingen Series LVI, New York: Pantheon.

Erikson, E.H. (1951) 'Sex differences in the play configuration of pre-adolescents', *American Journal of Orthopsychiatry* 21: 667–92.

—— (1964) 'Inner and outer space: reflections on womanhood', *Daedalus* 93: 558–97.

Evans, C. de B. (trans.) (1924) *Meister Eckhart*, by F. Pfeiffer (1857), Vol. 1. London: J.M. Watkins.

Fordham, M. (1944) *The Life of Childhood*, London: Routledge.

Freud, S. (1925) *Collected Papers*, vol. II, London: Hogarth.

—— (1927) *The Ego and the Id*, London: Hogarth.

Hubert, H. and Mauss, M. (1898) *Sacrifice in Nature and Function*, London: Cohen & West (see 1964 edn).

Jaffe, A. (1972) *From the Life and Work of C.G. Jung*, London: Hodder & Stoughton.

Jung, C.G. (1933) *Modern Man in Search of a Soul*, New York: Harcourt Brace.

—— (1939) 'Die psychologischen Aspekte des Muttersarchetypus', *Eranos Jahrbuch* 8: 79–91, Zürich: Eranos.

—— (1954a) *The Development of Personality*, Collected Works, vol. 17, London: Routledge.

117

—— (1954b) *The Practice of Psychotherapy, Collected Works*, vol. 16, London: Routledge.

—— (1956) *Symbols of Transformation, Collected Works*, vol. 5, London: Routledge.

—— (1959a) *The Archetypes of the Collective Unconscious, Collected Works*, vol. 9, part 1, London: Routledge.

—— (1959b) 'The concept of the collective unconscious', in *Collected Works*, vol. 9, part 1, London: Routledge.

—— (1960) *The Structure and Dynamics of the Psyche, Collected Works*, vol. 18, part 1, London: Routledge.

—— (1961a) *Two Essays on Analytical Psychology, Collected Works*, vol. 7, London: Routledge.

—— (1961b) *Freud and Psychoanalysis, Collected Works*, vol. 4, London: Routledge.

—— (1961c) *Memories, Dreams, Reflections*, New York: Panther Books.

—— (1969a) 'The holy men of India: introduction to Zimmer's *Der Weg zum Selbst*', in *Collected Works*, vol. 11, London: Routledge.

—— (1969b) *Psychology and Religion: West and East, Collected Works*, vol. 11, London: Routledge.

—— (1971) *Psychological Types, Collected Works*, vol. 6, London: Routledge.

—— (1972) *The Structure and Dynamics of the Psyche, Collected Works*, vol. 8, London: Routledge.

Kalff, D.M. (1980) *Sandplay* Boston: Sigo Press.

Krishna, G. (1972) *The Secret of Yoga*, London: Turnstone.

Lawrence, D.H. (1922) *Fantasia of the Unconscious*, New York: Seltzer.

Leenhardt, M. (1947) *De Kamo: Les Personnes et le Mythe du Monde Mélanésien*, Paris: Gallimard.

Lowenfeld, M. (1979) *The World Technique*, London: Allen & Unwin.

Luria, A.R. (1966) 'L.S. Vygotsky and the problem of functional localization', *Soviet Psychology* 5: 53–60.

McGuire, W. (ed.) (1974) *The Freud/Jung Letters*, Bollingen Series XCIV, Princeton: University Press.

Meier-Seethaler, C. (1982) 'Erich Neumann's contribution to the psychopathology of child development', *Journal of Analytical Psychology* 27(4): 357–79.

Miller, D.L. (1980) 'Theology's ego/religion's soul', *Spring*, 78–89.

Millar, S. (1968) *The Psychology of Play* London: Penguin.

Neumann, E. (1973) *The Child*, New York: G.P. Putnam's Sons.

Piaget, J. (1951) *Play, Dreams and Imitation in Childhood*, London: Routledge.

Rudin, J. (1968) *Psychotherapy and Religion*, London: Notre Dame Press.

Ryce-Menuhin, J. (1984) 'From the analysts' chair in 1984', *Harvest* 30: 89.

—— (1988) *The Self in Early Childhood*, London: Free Association Books.

Sardello, R. (1982) 'The Landscape of Virginity', in J. Stroud and G. Thomas (eds) *Images of the Untouched*, Dallas: Spring Publications.

Vygotsky, L.S. (1962) *Thought and Language*, E. Haufmann and G. Vakat (eds and trans.), New York: Wiley.

Watkins, M. (1981) 'Six approaches to the image in art therapy', *Spring*, Dallas: Spring Publications.

Weinrib, E.L. (1983) *Images of the Self*, Boston: Sigo Press.

Wells, H.G. (1911) *Floor Games,* New York: Arno Press (revised edn published in 1975).

Wilhelm, R. (1951) (trans.) *I Ching or Book of Changes,* London: Routledge.

Winnicott, D.W. (1971) *Playing and Reality* London: Tavistock.

NAME INDEX

Adler, Gerhard 49, 59
Aristotle 40

Bastian, Adolf 18
Böehme, J. 54
Brown, Albert 18
Budge, Sir E.H. Wallis 73
Burckhardt, Jacob 18

Coomaraswamy, A.K. 76–7

de Laszlo, Violet 1
de Vries, A. 24

Eckhart, Meister 76
Eichmann, Adolf 57
Eliade, Mircea 26
Erikson, Eric 4
Evans, C. de B. 76

Fordham, Michael 20, 46, 49
Freud, Anna 49
Freud, Sigmund 6, 7, 15–16, 17,
   19–20, 22–3, 47, 64

Graves, Robert 87

Hubert, H. 18

Jaffe, A. 16
Jalalu'd-Din Rumi 77
Jung, C.G. 2, 3, 4, 6–7, 33, 38, 40,
   46, 63, 64, 65, 89, 90; archetypal
   theory and symbols 15, 16–20,
   21, 22, 23, 48, 67, 79–80, 96

Jung, Emma 2, 4

Kalff, Dora 1–2, 3, 4, 23, 24, 25, 26,
   31, 33, 102, 106, 107–8, 110;
   correspondence with Margaret
   Lowenfeld 112–15
Kalff, Martin 107
Kalff, Sabina 107
Kernberg, Otto 49
Kohut, Heinz 49
Krishna, Gopi 26

Lawrence, D.H. 51
Layard, John 82
Leenhardt, Maurice 28
Leonardo da Vinci 17
Lowenfeld, Margaret 2, 3–4, 5–6;
   correspondence with Dora Kalff
   112–15
Luria, A.R. 8, 9

McGuire, W. 20
Marinucci, S. 97
Mauss, M. 18
Meier-Seethaler, C. 59
Millar, S. 9
Miller, D.L. 64
Montecchi, F. 97

Nagliero, G. 97
Neumann, E. 59

Piaget, J. 9, 10, 46
Plato 18, 76

120

Rudin, J. 65
Ryce-Menuhin, Joel 4, 8–10, 14,
    15–20, 45, 111, 116

Sardello, Robert 82
Schiller, Friedrich 7
Shakespeare, William 87
Stein, Leopold 49
Steiner, Rudolph 104

Tortolani, D. 97

Vygotsky, L.S. 9

Watkins, Mary 3
Weinrib, E.L. 2, 79
Wells, H.G. 3
Wilhelm, R. 106
Winnicott, D.W. 10, 21, 49, 52, 53,
    101

SUBJECT INDEX

accidents 103
achievement and masculinity 31
active imagination 19, 33
adolescence: case study 38, 77–89,
    Plates 24–33
adults: uses of sandplay for 103
affectivity 98; *see also* feeling
aggression, child 98, 99, 100, 101
agnostics 104
alchemy, alchemical process 55, 57,
    60, 104
alter-ego *see* shadow
analyst *see* therapist
analytical psychology *see* Jungian
    analysis
Analytical Psychology Club 23
angels in dreams and sandplay 56,
    72, 73–4, 76
anima: case study (1) 40, 42, 43, 44;
    case study (2) 38, 53, 54, 55, 58,
    61, 62, 63; and sandplay forms
    95–6
animals 60, 61, 62, 63, 67–76 *passim*,
    79, 80, 82, 83, 84, 86, 89; bull 87,
    88; horse *see* horses
animus: case study (1) 41; case
    study (2) 51; case study (3) 67,
    69, 70, 71; case study (4) 84, 87,
    88; and sandplay forms 95–6
anthropology 18, 19, 26
anxiety 77, 89
appearance: differentiation from
    reality 22
archetypal games 6

archetypal images 16, 17–18, 19–20,
    21, 22, 24–7, 30, 36–7, 46, 49, 60,
    62, 65, 101, 105, 106; of God 65,
    104
archetypes 15–20, 21, 22, 25, 26, 65,
    81, 96, 104; child 6, 18, 19, 36,
    41, 42, 43, 69, 90; earth mother
    19, 24; family unity 79; of
    meaning 67; parental 19, 48, 49,
    59; and sandplay forms 92–3;
    shadow *see* shadow; syzygy 19,
    81; wise old man 19, 42
astrology 26, 102
atheists 104
autistic children 29, 35, 102–3
autonomy 11–12, 88
awe 37

Ba 73
babies 30, 46–8, 52; *see also* children
baby as symbol 43, 44, 56
Babylonian mythology 61
Bambino Gesu Hospital, Milan 97
Bedford College, London 16
behaviour patterns 16
birds 43, 44, 67, 69, 70, 72, 74, 76,
    83, 84–5, 86
birth 98; trauma of 53, 56–7
bisexuals 35
boats 73, 74, 79, 82
bridges 60, 62, 80, 83, 84
British Sandplay Group 116
Buddha 70, 73, 74
buildings (sandplay objects) 5–6, 43

bulls 87, 88
butterflies 87

California: group experiments in 103
cancer patients: sandplay and diagnosis in 97–101
cars 83
carving 19
case studies: (1) A man maturing 38, 39–45, *Plates* 1–8; (2) A man healed of traumatic childhood ego damage 38, 45–65, *Plates* 9–12; (3) A woman in grief 33, 38, 66–77, *Plates* 13–23; (4) A girl entering puberty 38, 77–89, *Plates* 24–33
categories *see* archetypal images
catharsis 40, 56, 61
chaos 14, 35, 90
child abuse 103
child analysis 105
child archetype *see* archetypes
childhood: of Jung 6–7
childhood associations 7, 105
childhood fantasy 17, 21, 90
childhood traumata 39, 42, 45, 105
children: aggression 98, 99, 100, 101; autistic 29, 35, 102–3; and circus 113; depression 36; development 9–11, 65; diagnosis in cancer patients 97–101; obsessive 35, 98; and parental archetypes 19, 48, 49, 59; participation of therapist with 102–3; and play 4, 9–11; and play therapy 29–30; psyche 18; psychiatric treatment and emergence of 'World Technique' 3–4; and reality 21, 48; and transitional objects 10, 21, 101; value of sandplay for 6; *see also* babies
Chinese mythology 26, 44, 68
Christian figures and symbols 17, 23, 27, 32, 41, 42, 55, 68, 69, 72, 73, 74, 75
circus as symbol 113

civilization and play 8
clay modelling 19, 105
cognition 22, 48–9
collective unconscious 15–17, 26, 46, 47, 49, 65, 79, 81, 91–2, 94: *see also* archetypes
colours 26, 71, 83, 104
compensation 48
complex(es) 3, 54, 65; mother 42
concentration 14, 26, 102
concern, sense of 21
conflict 13, 14
Congress of Psychology, Paris (1937) 4
conscious 17, 25, 27, 91–2, 94; relationship with unconscious 22, 47, 65, 89
consciousness 17, 46, 47; expansion of 2–3, 4
conversation 102
counter-transference *see* transference and counter-transference
craft, sandplay as 106
creative imagination, creativity 6–7, 14
crystal: compared with collective unconscious 16, 79–80
cultural environment and traditions 105, 111; child and 49

death 67, 69, 72–3, 76, 77, 81, 98; and sandplay forms 100, 101; *see also* grief
defences 13, 14, 22–3, 35, 47, 64, 98, 102; case study (1) 39, 43; case study (2) 52, 59
deintegration 46
delusions 16, 17
depersonalization 52, 53
depression 30–1, 36, 52, 54, 55, 56, 69, 75, 98; author's, and its treatment 1, 31; case study (4) 77, 79, 81, 82, 87, 88
development, developmental problems 3, 38, 89, 103; *see also* children
diagnosis and sandplay 97–101
distress-ego 59, 60

Divine Mother (Mahasakti) 74, 75, 76
drawing 19
dream analysis 19, 20, 38
dream(s) 3, 7, 16, 17, 19, 20, 104; case study (2) 50, 51, 53–7, 60, 65; case study (4) 78, 79; myth as a 26
dual mother 17

earth mother 19, 24
Eastern *see* Oriental
Eden 101
educational psychology 89
ego 20, 21, 33; case study (1) 42, 43, 44, 45; case study (2) 50–63; case study (3) 67, 74; case study (4) 83, 84, 85; damage to 45, 49–63, 64; dissolution of 50; distress-ego 59, 60; Freud and 23; and religion 64–65; and sandplay forms 92–3, 95; theory 46–50
ego-centricity 43, 59, 115
ego-ideal 47–8, 49
ego-strengthening 89; case study (2) 63; case study (3) 76; and play 9–11
Egyptian civilization and mythology 17, 19, 25, 71, 72–3, 84, 87
emotional impact of sandplay 32, 40, 56, 61; *see also* feeling
envy 50
equipment for sandplay 109
Eros 31
Eternal Child *see* archetypes, child
ethnology 18, 19, 26
European heritage: symbol of 86
ewekë 28, 29
expansion of consciousness 2–3, 4
experience and play 10–11
extraversion 7; case study 38, 78, 85

factories: sandplay in 103
fair play, concept of 8
fairy tales 16, 20
family 79, 95

fantasy 6, 7, 17, 20, 33, 90, 101; child and 17, 21, 90; symbolic 9, 19, 89; *see also* imagination
father 42, 47, 48, 50; case study (4) 77–89 *passim*; *see also* parental caring, parents
Faust 18
feeling 4, 32; *see also* emotional impact of sandplay
feminine principle, femininity 24, 31, 69, 113; case study (2) 55; case study (4) 84, 85, 86
fertility 70, 80, 84, 85, 87
fixations 65
folklore 20, 26
free association 19
freedom 6, 13, 105; from self 77; *see also* spontaneity
Freudianism 30, 32, 114
frogs 42, 43, 70–1
frustration 59
future: projection of, during sandplay 2, 102

gates 62, 74, 75, 88, 107
Germanic legends 26
gestures 4
girl: case study of 38, 77–89, *Plates* 24–33
Gnosticism 24
God 31, 37, 49, 50, 65
God-image 65, 104
Great Mother 60, 71
Greek mythology 17, 24–5, 55, 87
grief 38, 42, 66–77; *see also* death
Grim Reaper 69, 70
groups for sandplay 103

hatred 50
healing: snake associated with processes of 24, 25
healing, psychological 2–3, 13, 20, 29, 32, 33, 70, 102, 105, 106; case study (3) 38, 71; case study (4) 88, 89
hieros gamos 75
horses 42, 60, 67, 69, 70, 71, 74, 75, 76, 81, 83, 84, 86, 112, 113
hysteria 35

I.C.P. 113, 114
I Ching 58, 106
ideas 89, 90
images 7; archetypal *see* archetypal images; non-verbal 2, 3, 12–13; religious 64, 65; symbolic 4, 16, 19, 22; *see also* symbols, symbolization
imagination: active 19, 33; and play 10–11, 30
Immortal Self 77
immortality 68, 72–3
independence 11–12, 88; *see also* separation
Indian chieftain and family 67, 69, 71, 74–5, 84
Indian mythology and literature 25, 75, 87–8
individuation 26, 39, 63, 64, 70, 74, 104
initiation 28, 29, 88, 102
innocence 86
insects 86, 87; and psychosis 34
instincts 17, 20, 23, 25, 47, 61, 89, 90, 113; gratification of 10
International Society for Sandplay Therapy 23, 97, 110, 116
interpretation 4, 5–6, 12, 15, 19, 20, 32, 33–4, 36, 89–90, 102; suspicion of 101; *see also* symbolic meanings, symbols, symbolization
introversion 7
intuition 4, 28, 32
intuitive reading of sandplay 102
Isaiah 90

Jung Institute, Küssnacht 107
Jungian analysis 15, 19, 46, 65, 95; sandplay used in conjunction with 2, 6, 33, 34, 97, 113, 115
Jungian psychotherapy 40; Confession 40, 41, *Plate 1*; Elucidation 40, 41–2, *Plates 2–4*; Education 40, 43, *Plate 5*; Transformation 40, 43–5, *Plates 6–8*
Jungians: conflicts between 114

Ka 72–3, 77
Khaibit 73
Khu 73
Kleinian play therapy 30
Knight 43, 44
knowledge 22
Kundalini 24, 25, 44, 75

lambs 68, 69
language 22; ambiguities of 12–13; *see also* speech; verbal
lateral thinking 106
legends 26
libido *see* psychic energy
Lifou language 28
London: conflicts between Jungians in 114
loneliness 70
love 70, 84
Lowenfeld Archives 112

mana possession, inflation 40, 43, 45, 50
mandala, mandala construction 62, 83, 95
marriage: case study involving 38, 39–45, *Plates 1–8*
masculine principle, masculinity 31, 95, 113; case study (2) 5; case study (4) 85
masturbation 52, 104
meaning: archetype of 67; and play in children 9
meanings: in life and religion 49, 64; symbolic *see* symbolic meanings
meditation 25
Melanesia 28
memories 7
men: case studies of 38, 39–65, plates 1–12; and sandplay therapy 4
menstruation 38, 77, 80, 82, 83, 88
mental laziness 63
mid-life crisis 2, 38
Mithraic cults 87
Moral Rearmament 55
mother 10, 47, 48, 50; case study (1) 41, 42; case study (2) 57–61

passim; case study (3) 71; case
    study (4) 77–89 *passim*; dual 17
mother complex 42
mourning *see* grief
music: listening to 13; sonata form
    parallel to stages of
    psychotherapy 40
mysticism 17
myth, person 7, 28
myths 16, 17, 18, 19, 20, 24–5, 26,
    44, 55, 61, 68, 71, 72–3, 75, 87–8,
    111

narcissism 50–9 *passim*, 63, 85
neurosis 17, 50, 52, 64, 65
non-sense 14
Norse mythology 24
numbers: three 69; five 75
numinosity 37, 76

object psyche *see* collective
    unconscious
obsessives 35, 98
occult philosophy 17
octopus 80
offices: sandplay in 103
orality 98, 99, 100
Oriental figures and imagery: case
    study (1) 44; case study (3)
    67–76 *passim*; case study (4) 79,
    82, 84, 86, 87, 88, 89
Oriental philosophy 25

painting 19, 105
paramahamra 69
parental caring, parents 10, 11, 19,
    47–8, 49–50, 52, 59, 77–89, 98
parental fantasies 100
patience 15, 36
patients: behaviour during
    sandplay 5, 97; curiosity about
    sandplay 35; interaction with
    sandplay 3, 4; non-rational
    expression 5; suitability for
    sandplay 4, 34–6; transference
    conflicts 33
perception 46; universal patterns of
    see archetypes

Persian mythology 25
persona 52, 53, 56, 85
personal unconscious 15, 17, 25, 81,
    91–2, 94, 106
phallic symbols 24, 41, 42, 86, 87,
    88
photography 5, 97, 106, 109, 114
physically handicapped 103
physics 15, 22
play 4; physical aspect 14;
    psychology of 8–11; symbolic 9,
    33, 90
play therapy 29–30
pre-verbal expression, level 3, 14,
    32, 81
prediction, sandplay used for 2, 102
primordial images *see* archetypal
    images
protection 5, 6, 12
psyche 17, 18, 19, 36, 46, 50, 103,
    104, 105; and fantasy 7; levels
    projected into sandplay 91–7;
    observation of 15; and symbolic
    play 22, 28–34 *passim*, 90, 106;
    and water symbolism 56, 106
psychiatric day centres 103
psychic development 106
psychic energy 31, 36, 40, 89, 90;
    case studies 42, 43, 60, 61, 69, 71
psychic impulses 101
psychic wholeness 6
psychodiagnosis 110
psychological change 3
psychologists: suspicion amongst
    101
psychology 111; analytical *see*
    Jungian analysis; educational 89
psychopathology 110
psychotherapy 110; Jungian *see*
    Jungian psychotherapy; and
    religion 45, 63, 64–5
psychotics, psychosis 34, 103
puberty: case study 38, 77–89,
    Plates 24–33
puer aeternus see archetypes, child
punishment 47, 50

rational thinking: discouraged in
    sand therapy 3

reaction formation 39
reality: child and 21, 48;
    differentiation from appearance
    22; and neurosis 64–5
rebirth 17, 37, 61, 68, 70, 76, 81, 98
reductive analysis, therapy 29–30,
    32, 89
regression 30, 32, 78, 98; and
    sandplay 3, 5, 13, 105
relationships: difficulties with 52,
    53, 63
religion 18, 26, 62, 111; and
    psychotherapy 45, 63, 64–5
religious expression in sandplay
    75–6, 104–5
repression 15, 16, 23, 47; case study
    (1) 39
reptiles 41, 43, 60, 76, 84, 86; and
    psychosis 34; snakes see snakes
rites de passage see initiation
ritual: obsessive 35; of sandplay 28,
    29, 31, 32, 36, 37, 103
Roman beliefs 86
rose, golden 86, 87
Royal Society of Medicine 23
royalty 55
rules of play 8, 10

sado-masochism 35, 61
sahu 72
Samadhi 26
sand as earth-medium 11, 104
sand pictures 4, 14; construction 5,
    12–13, 97; visual quality 12–13,
    106
sandplay: author's first experience
    of 1–2; equipment 109;
    frequency of use 32–3, 35, 36;
    Jung and 4, 6–7; origins and
    evolution of 2, 3–4; physical
    aspect 14, 106; statistical proofs
    97, 101; universality 105–6
sandplay forms: mapping 91–7
sandplay objects 29–30, 104, 109; in
    case studies 41–5, 60–3, 67–77,
    79–89; meanings see symbolic
    meanings; placement 93, 97
sandplay rooms 4, 29, 97, 103, 109;
    Dora Kalff's 1, 107

sandplay therapy: suitability for 4,
    34–6
sandtrays 4–5, 6, 35, 59, 109
schizophrenia 25, 50
science and imprint 18
security fears 47
Sekhem 73
self 20, 21, 28, 37, 46, 50, 77, 89,
    100; case study (1) 39, 44, 45;
    case study (2) 55, 62; case study
    (3) 69; damage to 101; limitation
    in play 8, 10; and religion 64;
    and sandplay forms 95, 96–7
self-confidence 11, 86
self-consciousness 78
self-discovery, knowledge 10–11,
    14, 28, 105; case study (2) 45;
    case study (3) 69; case study (4)
    85
self-expression 13, 29–30
self-interpretation: dangers of
    103–4
self-realization 28, 111
sensation 4
separation 11, 21, 66; see also
    independence
seriousness and play 9
sexual images and symbols 41, 42,
    43, 56, 60, 86, 87, 88, 104
sexual patterns and problems 50,
    52–3, 57, 63
sexuality 78, 84, 85, 86, 113
shadow 19, 21, 40, 41, 43, 53, 57, 63,
    99, 100
shells 62, 70, 80, 85, 86
signs 23
snakes 23–6, 44, 56, 75, 85
Society for Analytical Psychology
    114
sonata form: parallel to stages of
    psychotherapy 40
soul 64, 76, 82
space: delimited 6, 35, 59;
    immobility in 99, 100, 101;
    meditative 76; menace of 58–9;
    relativity of 15
space walks 46
speech 4, 12–13, 14, 97 see also
    verbal

spiritual expression in sandplay 75–6, 104–5
spontaneity 5, 102, 106, 111
Spring 3
stones, stone circles 42, 62, 70, 74, 76, 81, 85, 86
stress 89, 98
superstition 26
symbolic 3, 28
symbolic fantasy 9, 89
symbolic images 4, 16, 19, 22
symbolic meanings 3, 5–6, 19, 20, 33, 36; in case studies 41–5, 53–7, 60–3, 67–77, 79–89; *see also* interpretation
symbolic play 9, 33, 90; objects *see* sandplay objects
symbols, symbolization 4, 20, 21, 22–7, 90; child's learning 21; difficulty in 98; *see also* individual symbols
synthetic interpretation *see* interpretation
syzygy 19, 81

theology 64
therapist: alertness and sensitivity to images 3; interpretation by *see* interpretation; necessity of presence of 103–4; as observer 4, 6, 11, 32, 35, 36, 79, 106; participation with children in sandplay 102–3; patience 15, 36; and stages of construction 5; training 110–11
thought 4, 70; development of abstract 10; discouragement of rational, in sandplay 3
time: disturbed perception of, in cancer patients 99, 100, 101; relativity of 15; snakes symbolizing 25
tragedy 40
transcendent function 20–1, 89
transference and counter-transference 12, 33, 40, 57, 58, 83

transitional object 10, 21, 52, 101
trees 41, 42, 61, 69, 70, 71, 76, 82, 85, 86

unconscious 26, 67, 90; collective *see* collective unconscious; and Jung 7, 19, 23; personal 15, 16, 17, 25, 81, 91–2, 94, 106; projected in sandplay 3, 28, 103; related to conscious 22, 47, 65, 89; snake as symbol of borders of 24
uterus 43, 104

verbal analysis: accompanying sandplay 32, 33, 34, 36, 60, 79; author's experience of, with Dora Kalff 1
verbal feedback 102
verbal psychotherapy 3, 13, 32, 34, 35, 57, 59, 105–6; *see also* words
virginity 80, 82, 83

waiting quality 80, 82, 83
war 8
water: compared with psychic development 106; symbolism of 56, 67, 82
water jugs 109
wholeness, psychic 6
wisdom 85
wise old man 19, 42
women: case studies 33, 38, 66–89, *Plates* 13–33; psychoanalysis and sandplay 4
wonder 37
words 4, 12–13, 14, 97; *see also* verbal
work 10
working class: case study of 45–65
'World Technique' of Margaret Lowenfeld 3–4, 112, 113

Yahweh *see* God
yoga 26

Zurich: analysts trained in 114; author's visit to home of Dora Kalff 1, 107–8